用 英 语 介 绍 中 国

# TALK ABOUT CHINESE CULTURE IN ENGLISH

# 用英语介绍中国文化

卓燃 著

化学工业出版社

·北京·

**图书在版编目(CIP)数据**

用英语介绍中国文化：英、汉 / 卓燃著. -- 北京：化学工业出版社, 2025.1 (2025.6重印). -- (用英语介绍中国). ISBN 978-7-122-46626-6

Ⅰ. K203-49

中国国家版本馆CIP数据核字第202456DE67号

责任编辑：马　骄　马小桐　　　　　装帧设计：张　辉
责任校对：边　涛　　　　　　　　　　版式设计：梧桐影

出版发行：化学工业出版社
　　　　　（北京市东城区青年湖南街13号　邮政编码100011）
印　　装：北京瑞禾彩色印刷有限公司
787mm×1092mm　1/16　印张12　字数227千字
2025年6月北京第1版第7次印刷

购书咨询：010-64518888　　　　　　售后服务：010-64518899
网　　址：http://www.cip.com.cn
凡购买本书，如有缺损质量问题，本社销售中心负责调换。

定　价：69.90元　　　　　　　　　　　　　　　版权所有　违者必究

# 目录

## Part 1　中国的**历史文化**

| | | |
|---|---|---|
| The Imperial Palace | 故宫：中国的永恒瑰宝 | 002 |
| The Terracotta Warriors | 兵马俑：宏伟的"地下军团" | 008 |
| The Mogao Grottoes | 莫高窟：大漠中的艺术宫殿 | 013 |
| The Great Wall | 长城：蜿蜒的万里巨龙 | 019 |
| The Summer Palace | 颐和园：感受皇家园林的魅力 | 025 |
| The Yungang Grottoes | 云冈石窟：巧夺天工的雕刻艺术 | 031 |
| Fujian Tulou | 福建土楼：独具特色的建筑艺术 | 037 |
| Suzhou Classical Gardens | 苏州古典园林：东方园林的精致之美 | 043 |
| Pingyao Ancient City | 平遥古城：跨越千年的城市 | 049 |
| The Temple of Heaven | 天坛：中国古代哲学思想的体现 | 055 |

## Part 2　中国的**经典艺术**

| | | |
|---|---|---|
| Peking Opera | 京剧：当之无愧的"国粹" | 062 |
| Chinese Painting | 国画：独特的东方韵味 | 068 |
| Porcelain | 瓷器：让世界感到精湛的技艺 | 074 |
| Tang and Song Poetry | 唐诗宋词：中国传统的诗歌艺术 | 081 |
| Chinese Calligraphy | 书法：超越文字魅力的艺术 | 087 |
| Chinese Tea Culture | 茶文化：悠闲的生活艺术 | 092 |

| Chinese Silk | 丝绸：柔软高贵的典范 | 098 |
| Chinese Paper-cut | 剪纸艺术：民间艺术的代表 | 104 |

# Part 3 中国的传统节日和节气

| The Spring Festival | 春节：辞旧迎新又一年 | 111 |
| The Lantern Festival | 元宵节：团团圆圆的节日 | 117 |
| The Tomb-sweeping Day | 清明节：祭祖踏青的好时节 | 123 |
| The Dragon Boat Festival | 端午节：一起来赛龙舟吧 | 129 |
| The Mid-Autumn Festival | 中秋节：每逢佳节倍思亲 | 135 |
| Twenty-four Solar Terms | 二十四节气：中国古代智慧结晶 | 141 |

# Part 4 中国的现代科技和文化

| China Railway Highspeed | 中国高铁：有趣又快速的出行体验 | 148 |
| China's Space Exploration | 中国的太空探索：追寻星辰大海 | 154 |
| Digital Life in China | 数字生活在中国：一种新的生活方式 | 161 |
| New Energy Vehicles | 新能源汽车：驶向未来 | 167 |
| Artificial Intelligence (AI) | 人工智能：未来就在眼前 | 173 |

**参考答案**     179

# Part 1
# 中国的历史文化

# The Imperial Palace
## 故宫：中国的永恒瑰宝

**Listening & practice** 听英文原声，完成练习

▶扫码听音频◀

1. **Where is the Imperial Palace located?**
   A. In London
   B. In Beijing
   C. In New York

2. **Why is the Imperial Palace called the "Forbidden City"?**
   A. Because it was always locked.
   B. Because only the emperor could allow people to enter or leave.
   C. Because it was built on forbidden land.

3. **How long did it take to build the Imperial Palace?**
   A. 10 years
   B. 14 years
   C. 20 years

4. **Which is one of the most exciting parts of the Imperial Palace?**
   A. The Palace of Versailles
   B. The Hall of Supreme Harmony
   C. The Great Wall

5. **Why is the Imperial Palace important for the whole world?**
   A. Because it's a World Cultural Heritage site (世界文化遗产).
   B. Because it is very big.
   C. Because it is made of gold.

## Reading 阅读下面的文章

Have you ever wondered what it would be like to live in a palace? In Beijing, China, there is a **special** place called the **Forbidden** City (the Imperial Palace) where emperors once lived. Let's take a fun journey to discover the wonders of this ancient palace!

This palace is more than 600 years old! It started being built in 1406 and took 14 years to **finish**. In the past, 24 **emperors** lived there. They were from the Ming and Qing Dynasties. The palace was called the Forbidden City because, in the past, no one was **allowed** to enter or leave without the emperor's **permission**.

One of the most exciting parts is the Hall of Supreme Harmony. This is the biggest and most **important** building in the Imperial Palace. Here, emperors held grand ceremonies (典礼), met with important people, and made big decisions.

As you walk through the Imperial Palace, you will see beautiful gardens, lovely ponds, and **neat** bridges. There is even a special garden called the Imperial Garden where the emperor and his family would relax and enjoy nature. The garden has rocks of different shapes, ancient trees, and colourful flowers that make it a peaceful place to visit.

The Imperial Palace is also filled with amazing treasures. You can see ancient paintings, beautiful porcelain, and shiny jewelry. Each item tells a story about the rich history and culture of China. Some treasures are more than a thousand years old!

It's not just a **palace**; it's also a World Cultural **Heritage** site. That means it's very important for the whole world! People come from many places to see it and learn about China's history and culture.

Today, the Imperial Palace has become China's greatest museum-the Palace Museum which receives innumerable visitors every day.

Learning about the Imperial Palace helps us know about China's past and all the beautiful art and culture. We should feel happy to know about this special place and remember to **take care of** it so more people can see it in the future.

## Vocabulary and phrases 词汇和短语

special ['speʃl] 形 特殊的，特别的

finish ['fɪnɪʃ] 动 完成

allow [ə'laʊ] 动 容许

important [ɪm'pɔːtnt] 形 重要的

palace ['pæləs] 名 宫殿；王室

take care of 短 照顾

forbidden [fə'bɪdn] 形 被禁止的

emperor ['empərə(r)] 名 皇帝；帝王

permission [pə'mɪʃn] 名 许可；同意

neat [niːt] 形 整洁的；精致的

heritage ['herɪtɪdʒ] 名 遗产

## Practice 请选择合适的词填在下方的横线上

important    take care of    allowed    World    emperors

1. In the past, people were not _____ to enter the Forbidden City without the emperor's permission.

2. The emperor met _____ people and made big decisions in the Hall of Supreme Harmony.

3. The Imperial Palace became a _____ Cultural Heritage site.

4. In the past, 24_____ lived in the Imperial Palace.

5. We should remember to _____ the Imperial Palace.

## Talking practice 情景对话模拟练习

爱丽丝和汤姆正在谈论关于故宫的话题,你能跟着一起练习这段对话吗?

**Alice爱丽丝:** Hey, Tom! Did you visit the Imperial Palace in Beijing?
嗨,汤姆,你去北京的故宫了吗?

**Tom汤姆:** Yes, I did! The Imperial Palace is really great. It's so big and old!
是的,我去了!故宫真的很棒,它很大也很有历史!

**Alice爱丽丝:** Why is it called the Forbidden City?
为什么叫紫禁城呢?

**Tom汤姆:** Because, in the past, no one was allowed to enter or leave without the emperor's permission.
这是因为在过去,没有皇帝的许可,任何人都不能进出。

**Alice爱丽丝:** Wow, that's interesting! How old is the Imperial Palace?
哇,这太有趣了!故宫有多古老呢?

**Tom汤姆:** It's more than 600 years old. It was built in 1406 and 24 emperors lived there.
它有超过600年的历史,始建于1406年,有24个皇帝住过那里。

**Alice爱丽丝:** What can you see inside the Imperial Palace?
你在故宫里能看见什么?

Tom汤姆

There are many rooms with red walls and yellow roofs, and you can see lots of beautiful artworks. There are even pretty gardens with old trees.
故宫里面很多的房子，红墙黄瓦，你还能看到很多美丽的艺术品，甚至是漂亮的花园和古老的树。

I'd love to see that!
我真想去看看！

Alice爱丽丝

### Funny facts　关于故宫的有趣事实和短语

**龙的象征**：故宫中有超过一万个龙的图案，因为龙在中国文化中象征着皇权和尊贵。
**谜一样的数字"9"**：在中国文化中，数字"9"代表着长久和永恒，故宫的设计中处处可见"9"的痕迹，如紫禁城的大门钉，一般是9行9列。
**巧妙的防火系统**：为防止火灾，故宫内设置了大量的铜制水桶和水井。

| | |
|---|---|
| **moat** – 护城河 | **The Inner Court** – 内廷 |
| **The Meridian Gate** – 午门 | **The Outer Court** – 外朝 |
| **The Hall of Supreme Harmony** – 太和殿 | **The Imperial Garden** – 御花园 |
| | **The Golden Water Bridge** – 金水桥 |

### Writing practice　写作小练习

**根据我们这一节所学到的内容，写出下面句子的英文。**

1. 北京的故宫很大，里面有很多的房间。

   _____

2. 故宫修建于600多年前，它是中国的文化遗产。

   _____

3. 在故宫里，你会看到很多美丽的艺术品，以及漂亮的花园和古老的树木。

   _____

## Reference translation 参考译文

你有没有想过住在宫殿里是什么感觉？在中国的北京，有一个叫作紫禁城（故宫）的独特地方，这里曾是皇帝居住的地方。让我们一起开启一段有趣的旅程，来发现这个古老宫殿的奇妙之处吧！

这座宫殿已有六百多年的历史！它始建于1406年，历时14年才得以完工。在过去，有24位皇帝曾在此居住。他们分别来自明朝和清朝。这个宫殿之所以叫作"紫禁城"，是因为在过去，没有皇帝的许可，任何人都不能进出。

故宫最令人激动的部分之一是太和殿。这是故宫里最大最重要的建筑。在这里，皇帝举行盛大的仪式、会见重要人物，并做出重大决策。

走在故宫里面，你会看到美丽的花园、可爱的池塘和精致的桥梁。这里还有一个特别的花园叫作御花园，皇帝和他的家人在这里放松和享受自然。花园里有奇形怪状的岩石、古老的树木和五彩缤纷的花朵，使这里成为一个宁静的地方。

故宫里也有许多令人惊叹的珍宝。你可以看到古代的绘画、美丽的瓷器和闪亮的珠宝。每件物品都讲述了中国丰富历史和文化的故事。有些珍宝已有一千多年的历史！

它不仅仅是一座宫殿，还是世界文化遗产。这意味着它对全世界都非常重要！来自世界各地的人们都会来到这里，欣赏它并学习中国的历史和文化。

今天，这座皇宫已经成为中国最大的博物馆——故宫博物院，每天接待数不清的游客。

了解故宫有助于我们了解中国的过去以及所有美丽的艺术和文化。我们应该为了解这个特别的地方而感到高兴，并记住要保护它，以便未来更多的人可以看到它。

# The Terracotta Warriors
# 兵马俑：宏伟的"地下军团"

**Listening & practice** 听英文原声，完成练习

▶扫码听音频◀

1. **Who was the first emperor of China?**
   A. Emperor Qin Shi Huang
   B. Emperor Han Wu
   C. Emperor Tang Shen

2. **What did the workers build for Emperor Qin Shi Huang over 2,200 years ago?**
   A. A school
   B. A tomb (墓穴)
   C. A bridge

3. **What are the Terracotta Warriors made of?**
   A. Wood
   B. Stone
   C. Clay

4. **What unique feature do the Terracotta Warriors have?**
   A. They are all the same.
   B. They have different faces and hairstyles.
   C. They are very small.

5. **How were the Terracotta Warriors discovered in 1974?**
   A. During a government excavation (政府挖掘)
   B. By a farmer digging a well
   C. By a group of tourists

## Reading 阅读下面的文章

The Terracotta Warriors are special statues found near a city called Xi'an in China. A long time ago, they were made to protect the tomb of the first emperor of China, Emperor Qin Shi Huang.

Over 2,200 years ago, the emperor wanted a big tomb for himself, so he had over 700,000 workers build it for many years. They also made lots of soldier and horse statues out of clay.

There are many different Terracotta Warriors, like foot soldiers, horse riders, and chariots. These statues are almost as big as real people and they look very real! Each one has different face and hair style, which shows just how skilled the people who made them were.

The statues used to be colourful, but the colours have faded over time. They still look very real and strong, and they help us learn about what the emperor's army looked like a long time ago.

The emperor's tomb is very big, and the warriors are just one part of it. There were also weapons, jewellery, and other treasures found with them, which tells us the emperor wanted his tomb to be as grand as his palace.

The Terracotta Warriors were found in 1974 by a farmer who was just digging a well. This amazing find made many archaeologists (考古学家) come to learn more, and they dug up the area to find this hidden army of statues.

Because they are so special and old, the Terracotta Warriors are protected as a World Heritage Site. Every year, lots of people visit to see them and learn about old China. They are very important to China and the whole world.

## Vocabulary and phrases 词汇和短语

statue ['stætʃuː] 名 雕像

tomb [tuːm] 名 坟墓

clay [kleɪ] 名 黏土

soldier ['səʊldʒə(r)] 名 士兵

colourful ['kʌləfəl] 形 多彩的

warrior ['wɒriə(r)] 名 战士;勇士

treasure [ˈtreʒə(r)] 名 宝藏

protect [prəˈtekt] 动 保护

grand [grænd] 形 壮观的；伟大的

## Practice 请选择合适的词填在下方的横线上

statue　　treasures　　protect　　grand　　tomb

1. Every warrior _____ has a unique face.
2. Many old _____ were discovered with the warriors.
3. Strong walls _____ the emperor's tomb.
4. The emperor's tomb was as _____ as a palace.
5. The site includes the emperor's _____ surrounded by many statues.

## Talking practice 情景对话模拟练习

艾利克斯和莎拉正在谈论兵马俑，请你跟着练习这段对话吧。

Hey Sarah, have you heard about the Terracotta Warriors?
嘿，莎拉，你听说过兵马俑吗？

Alex艾利克斯

Sarah莎拉

Yes, I know that they are old statues found near Xi'an in China. What are they exactly?
是的，我知道它们是在中国西安附近发现的古老雕像。它们到底是什么？

They are clay statues of soldiers and horses made to protect the tomb of the first emperor of China, Emperor Qin Shi Huang.
它们是用黏土制成的士兵和马的雕像，用来保护中国第一位皇帝秦始皇的墓。

Alex艾利克斯

Sarah莎拉

That's interesting! How old are they?
真有意思！它们有多古老？

They're over 2,200 years old. A farmer found them by accident in 1974 while digging a well.
它们有2,200多年历史了。1974年，一位农民挖井时偶然发现了它们。

Alex艾利克斯

Sarah莎拉

Wow, that's quite a discovery! How many statues are there?
哇，这真是个了不起的发现！那里有多少个雕像？

There are thousands of them, including foot soldiers, horse riders, and chariots. Each one looks different with unique faces and hairstyles.
有成千上万个，包括步兵、骑兵和马车。每一个都看起来不同，有独特的面孔和发型。

Alex艾利克斯

Sarah莎拉

It must be amazing to see them. I hope I can visit them someday!
亲眼看到它们一定很棒。我希望有一天能去参观！

## Funny facts  关于兵马俑的有趣事实和短语

**个性十足的雕像**：每个兵马俑的面孔都是独一无二的，表情、发型甚至服装细节都各不相同，展示了古代工匠的精湛技艺。

**彩绘的秘密**：兵马俑原来是五彩缤纷的，每个雕像都涂有鲜艳的颜色。但由于时间流逝和氧化作用，这些颜色已经褪去。

**不只是士兵**：除了步兵、骑兵外，兵马俑还包括了文官和武将雕像，形成了一个完整的地下军事体系。

| | |
|---|---|
| the First Emperor – 第一位皇帝（指秦始皇） | bronze sword – 青铜剑 |
| Qin Dynasty – 秦朝 | crossbow – 弩 |
| the Mausoleum of the Emperor Qin Shi Huang – 秦始皇帝陵 | armor – 盔甲 |
| | archaeological site – 考古遗址 |

## Writing practice 写作小练习

根据我们这一节所学到的内容,写出下面句子的英文。

1. 这些士兵和马都是由黏土制成的。
   ___

2. 秦始皇的陵墓非常宏伟。
   ___

3. 在1974年,一位农民发现了兵马俑。
   ___

## Reference translation 参考译文

兵马俑是中国西安附近发现的特殊雕像。很久以前,它们是为了保护中国第一位皇帝秦始皇的陵墓而制作的。

在2,200多年前,这位皇帝希望为自己建造一座宏大的陵墓,于是他命令超过70多万名工匠,花费了许多年的时间修建了这个皇陵。他们还制作了大量用黏土制成的士兵和马匹雕像。

兵马俑种类繁多,包括步兵、骑兵以及马车。这些雕像几乎与真人一般大小,看起来栩栩如生!每一个兵马俑的面孔和发型都是独一无二的,显示出当时工匠们极高的技艺。

这些雕像曾经是色彩斑斓的,但因为时间的流逝,它们的颜色已经褪去了。尽管如此,它们仍然看起来非常逼真且气势磅礴,帮助我们了解很久以前皇帝军队的模样。

秦始皇的陵墓非常宏伟,兵马俑只是其中的一部分。这里还有武器、珠宝和其他艺术品,这些发现表明秦始皇希望自己的墓地就像他活着时的皇宫一样壮观。

1974年,一位农民在挖井时意外发现了兵马俑。这一神奇的发现吸引了很多考古学家们前来研究,他们在这个地方深入挖掘出了这个隐藏的军团。

由于兵马俑的独特性和古老性,它们被列为世界遗产并受到保护。每年都有大量游客前来参观,了解古老的中国。兵马俑对中国乃至全世界都具有重要意义。

# The Mogao Grottoes
## 莫高窟：大漠中的艺术宫殿

**Listening & practice**  听英文原声，完成练习

▶扫码听音频◀

1. Where are the Mogao Grottoes located?
   A. Beijing
   B. Shanghai
   C. Dunhuang

2. Who dug the first cave at Mogao?
   A. A king
   B. A monk named Lezun
   C. A farmer

3. What can you find inside the Mogao Grottoes?
   A. Colourful paintings and statues
   B. Modern art
   C. Gold and silver

4. What do the paintings in the Mogao Grottoes mainly show?
   A. Stories about Buddha and ancient life
   B. Maps of China
   C. Pictures of animals

5. Why are the Mogao Grottoes considered (被认为) special and important?
   A. They are a World Heritage site.
   B. They are the tallest buildings in the world.
   C. They have gold inside.

## Reading 阅读下面的文章

The Mogao Grottoes are a magical place in Dunhuang City, Gansu Province, China. They are in the middle of pretty deserts and are full of ancient grottoes called the "Treasure House of Eastern Art."

A very long time ago, around 1,600 years back, a monk named Lezun dug the first grotto to pray and find peace. After that, many people added beautiful paintings and statues to show what life and beliefs were like back then.

There are 767 grottoes at Mogao, and they all have colourful paintings on the walls and ceilings. These paintings share stories about Buddha and life in ancient times. Every grotto has its own style and story, making each one feel like a different little world.

The Mogao Grottoes are designed in a special way. Some grottoes have a big room with a large Buddha statue in the middle and many smaller statues around it. The statues look very real and show how good the old artists were.

The art in Mogao Grottoes is so important that many artists and visitors come to see and learn from it. In 1990, UNESCO named the Mogao Grottoes a World Heritage Site, which means they are very important and special.

Every year, lots of children and their families visit the Mogao Grottoes. It's a perfect place to learn about ancient Chinese culture and art, and it helps us understand why it's important to protect old treasures.

## Vocabulary and phrases 词汇和短语

grotto [ˈgrɒtəʊ] 名 洞窟

eastern [ˈiːstən] 形 东方的

pray [preɪ] 动 祈祷

ceiling [ˈsiːlɪŋ] 名 天花板

design [dɪˈzaɪn] 动 设计

culture [ˈkʌltʃə(r)] 名 文化

magical [ˈmædʒɪkl] 形 魔法的；神奇的

monk [mʌŋk] 名 和尚

belief [bɪˈliːf] 名 信仰

Buddha [ˈbʊdə] 名 佛；佛像

UNESCO [juːˈneskəʊ] 缩 联合国教科文组织

## Practice 请选择合适的词填在下方的横线上

monk    designed    magical    UNESCO    eastern

1. The Mogao Grottoes are famous for their _____ art styles in the paintings.

2. The Mogao Grottoes were recognized by _____ as a World Heritage Site.

3. The first grotto was dug by a _____ who wanted a quiet place to pray.

4. The grottoes are _____ with a large Buddha statue in the centre of each main room.

5. The Mogao Grottoes are described as a _____ place full of history and art.

## Talking practice 情景对话模拟练习

一位导游正在向游客介绍莫高窟,你能跟着练习这段对话吗?

Welcome to the Mogao Grottoes, a very special place in China.
欢迎来到莫高窟,中国一个非常特别的地方。

Tour Guide导游

Visitor游客

How old are these grottoes?
这些洞穴有多古老?

A monk started the first grotto around 1,600 years ago.
一个和尚在约1,600年前开始挖掘出第一个洞穴。

Tour Guide导游

Visitor游客

Why are there paintings and statues everywhere?
为什么到处都是画和雕像?

People added them over many years to share their life and beliefs.
多年来人们添加了这些画和雕像,以分享他们的生活和信仰。

Tour Guide导游

Visitor游客

Wow, that's amazing.
哇,太棒了。

Yes, because of their great history and art, the Mogao Grottoes are a UNESCO World Heritage Site.
是的。由于这些伟大的历史和艺术,莫高窟成为了联合国教科文组织认定的世界文化遗产。

Tour Guide导游

Visitor游客

That's wonderful! We really should protect them better!
太伟大了!我们真应该更好地保护它们!

## Funny facts 关于莫高窟的有趣事实和短语

**敦煌飞天**：指敦煌石窟中的飞神，后来成为中国敦煌壁画艺术的一个专用名词。

**数字化保护**：为了保护脆弱的壁画不受游客影响，莫高窟部分洞窟对公众关闭。同时，科研团队利用高科技手段进行数字化保存，人们可以通过虚拟现实技术在线上欣赏这些壁画和雕塑。

**千佛洞**：莫高窟又称"千佛洞"，因为很多洞窟内都有佛像的绘画或雕刻，这些形象的风格各不相同，展示了不同时期的审美和技术特点。

| | |
|---|---|
| **buddhist art** – 佛教艺术 | **flying apsaras** – 飞天 |
| **wall paintings** – 壁画 | **the Nine-storied** – 九层楼 |
| **silk road** – 丝绸之路 | **the Three-storied** – 三层楼 |
| **grotto art** – 石窟艺术 | **Sutra Depository** – 藏经阁 |

## Writing practice 写作小练习

**根据我们这一节所学到的内容，写出下面句子的英文。**

1. 中国的莫高窟是一个神奇的地方。

   _____

2. 莫高窟里有很多古老且颜色丰富的绘画。

   _____

3. 每一年，有很多的游客探访莫高窟。

   _____

## Reference translation 参考译文

莫高窟是中国甘肃省敦煌市的一处神奇之地。它位于美丽的沙漠之中,遍布着被称为"东方艺术宝库"的古老洞穴。

很久很久以前,大约在1,600年前,一位名叫乐尊的和尚在这里挖掘了第一个石窟,用来祈祷和修行。后来,越来越多的人在这里留下壁画和雕塑,展示了当时人们的生活和信仰。

莫高窟共有767个洞穴,每个洞穴的墙壁和天花板上都绘有色彩斑斓的壁画。这些壁画讲述了佛祖和古代生活的故事。每个洞穴都有其独特的风格和故事,使每个洞穴仿佛是一个不同的小世界。

莫高窟的设计别具一格。一些洞穴在一个宽敞的空间中央矗立着一尊巨大的佛像,周围环绕着许多较小的雕像。这些雕像栩栩如生,展现了古代艺术家的精湛技艺。

莫高窟的艺术如此重要,以至于许多艺术家和游客前来参观并从中学习。1990年,联合国教科文组织将莫高窟列为世界文化遗产,这意味着它们具有非常重要的特殊意义。

每年,有很多小朋友和他们的家人来参观莫高窟。这里不仅是了解中国古代文化和艺术的好地方,也让我们学到了保护古老珍宝的重要性。

# The Great Wall
长城：蜿蜒的万里巨龙

## Listening & practice  听英文原声，完成练习

1. **Why was the Great Wall of China built?**
   A. To look beautiful
   B. To keep China safe from attackers (攻击者)
   C. To build houses

2. **Who made the Great Wall bigger and stronger?**
   A. The Ming Dynasty
   B. Emperor Qin Shi Huang
   C. Western Zhou Dynasty

3. **What was used to build the Great Wall?**
   A. Gold
   B. Wood
   C. Stones and bricks

4. **Why were there watchtowers on the Great Wall?**
   A. For parties
   B. For messages
   C. For decoration (装饰)

5. **When was the Great Wall named a World Heritage Site?**
   A. 1987
   B. 1990
   C. 1980

## Reading 阅读下面的文章

The Great Wall of China is one of the most famous buildings in the world. It is very old and looks amazing! A long time ago, the Great Wall was built to keep central plains safe from attackers coming from the north.

The building of the Great Wall started during the Western Zhou Dynasty, a really long time ago, before year zero! Over the next few centuries, different Chinese dynasties added to and fixed up the Wall.

The most famous part was built by the first emperor of China, Emperor Qin Shi Huang. After he brought all of China together, he made the Great Wall bigger and stronger to keep enemies out. The last big changes were made during the Ming Dynasty, and what we see mostly today comes from that time.

The Great Wall twists and turns and is over 21,000 kilometres long! It goes over mountains, through deserts, and across grasslands—it's really something to see! The Wall was built using lots of stones and bricks. Each part of the Wall was made using what was around, so every piece looks a bit different.

On the Great Wall, there are watchtowers along the way. What were these for? Back in old times, it was hard to send messages, so people used these watchtowers to send military messages and warnings. Soldiers would light fires on the watchtowers, and the smoke and light signals would send messages quickly.

The Great Wall isn't just a symbol of China; it's also a World Heritage Site. In 1987, the United Nations (联合国) said it was so special that it got added to the World Heritage List. This means the Great Wall is important not just to China, but to everyone in the world. You might have seen the Great Wall in movies or books—it helps people learn about Chinese history and culture.

I hope one day you can visit the Great Wall, too. You can stand on it and feel how big and old it is, and learn more about this amazing building's stories!

## Vocabulary and phrases 词汇和短语

attacker [ə'tækə(r)] 名 侵略者；攻击者

century ['sentʃəri] 名 世纪

enemy ['enəmi] 名 敌人

watchtower ['wɒtʃtaʊə(r)] 名 烽火台；瞭望塔

warning ['wɔːnɪŋ] 名 警告

dynasty ['dɪnəsti] 名 朝代

fix up 短 修理，整修

grassland ['ɡrɑːslænd] 名 草原

message ['mesɪdʒ] 名 信息；短信

symbol ['sɪmbl] 名 符号，象征

## Practice 请选择合适的词填在下方的横线上

> dynasty    fixed up    enemies    messages    symbol

1. Soldiers would light fires on the watchtowers, and the smoke and light signals would send _____ quickly.

2. The Great Wall isn't just a _____ of China; it's also a World Heritage Site.

3. Over the next few centuries, different Chinese dynasties added to and _____ the Wall.

4. The building of the Great Wall started during the Western Zhou _____.

5. Emperor Qin Shi Huang built the Great Wall to keep out _____.

## Talking practice 情景对话模拟练习

汤姆和玛丽正在谈论关于长城的话题,你能跟着一起练习这段对话吗?

Hey, Mary, did you know the Great Wall of China was originally built to protect central plains from northern attackers?
嘿,玛丽,你知道中国的长城最初是为了保护中原免受北方侵略者的攻击而建的吗?

Tom汤姆

Mary玛丽

Really? That's interesting! How old is the Great Wall?
真的吗?那很有趣!长城有多老?

It started during the Western Zhou Dynasty, way before the year zero.
它始建于西周时期,远在公元之前。

Tom汤姆

Mary玛丽

I heard the most famous part was built by Emperor Qin Shi Huang. Is that true?
我听说最著名的部分是由秦始皇建造的。这是真的吗?

Yes, he expanded the Wall to keep the enemies out after unifying China.
是的,他在统一中国后扩建了长城,以防止敌人进入。

Tom汤姆

Mary玛丽

And what about those watchtowers? What were they used for?
那些烽火台塔呢?它们是用来做什么的?

长城：蜿蜒的万里巨龙　023

They were used for sending military signals with fire and smoke to convey messages quickly across distances.
它们被用来以火和烟发出军事信号，以便迅速传递信息。

Tom汤姆

Mary玛丽

That's amazing! The Great Wall is not just a wall; it's a piece of living history!
太神奇了！长城不仅仅是一堵墙；它是活生生的历史！

## Funny facts　关于长城的有趣事实和短语

**总长度惊人**：长城的总长度超过2万公里。最著名的部分是明朝建造的长城，这部分长城的主要长度约为8,851公里。

**非连续结构**：虽然常被视为一道连续的长墙，实际上长城由多段墙体和防御工事组成，这些部分根据地理和战略需求分布在不同地区。

**防御系统复杂**：长城不仅仅是一堵墙，它包括了城墙、烽火台、兵站、关隘和堡垒。烽火台是长城的一个重要特点，用于传递军事情报。

---

Ming Dynasty Great Wall – 明长城
watchtowers on the Great Wall – 长城烽火台
Simatai Great Wall – 司马台长城
Jinshanling Great Wall – 金山岭长城
Mutianyu Great Wall – 慕田峪长城
Badaling Great Wall – 八达岭长城
heavenly ladder – 天梯
the First Pass Under Heaven – 天下第一关
brick by brick – 一砖一瓦

## Writing practice　写作小练习

根据我们这一节所学到的内容，写出下面句子的英文。

1. 长城是中国的代表符号。

2. 长城的总长度超过了2万公里。

———————————————————————————

3. 长城上的烽火台是用来传递信号的。

———————————————————————————

## Reference translation 参考译文

中国的长城是世界上最著名的建筑之一。它有非常悠久的历史，而且非常壮观。很久以前，长城是为了保护中原免受北方来犯之敌的侵扰而建造的。

长城的建造始于西周时期，那真是很久很久以前，远在公元元年之前！在接下来的几个世纪中，不同的朝代都对长城进行了增建和修缮。

其中最著名的一段是由中国第一位皇帝秦始皇建造的。在他统一中国之后，他将长城建得更大更坚固，以抵御外敌。最后一次大的改动发生在明朝，而我们今天所看到的长城大多源自那个时期。

长城蜿蜒曲折，全长超过21,000公里！它翻山越岭，穿越沙漠，横跨草原——真是一大奇观！长城是用大量的石头和砖块建造的。长城的每一部分都是就地取材建造的，所以每一块都略有不同。

在长城上，沿途设有烽火台。这是做什么用的呢？在古时候，人们通信并不方便，就用烽火台来传递军情和警报。士兵们可以在烽火台上点火，通过烟雾和火光信号快速传递信息。

长城不仅是中国的象征，也是世界文化遗产。1987年，联合国宣布其如此特别，并将其列入世界遗产名录。这标志着长城不仅对中国，对全世界都有重要的价值。长城也常常出现在电影和书籍中，成为人们了解中国历史和文化的一个窗口。

我希望有一天你也能参观长城。你可以站在上面，感受它的宏伟和古老，并了解更多关于这座神奇建筑的故事！

# The Summer Palace
颐和园：感受皇家园林的魅力

## Listening & practice  听英文原声，完成练习

▶扫码听音频◀

1. When was the Summer Palace first built?
   A. 1950
   B. 1750
   C. 1850

2. Why did Emperor Qianlong build the Summer Palace?
   A. For his vacation
   B. To celebrate his mother's birthday
   C. To meet friends

3. What is special about the Seventeen-Arch Bridge (十七孔桥)?
   A. It is very short.
   B. It is made of wood.
   C. It has many stone lions.

4. What can you see on the Long Corridor (长廊)?
   A. Only pictures of birds
   B. Chinese paintings of landscapes and figures
   C. Modern art

5. What is Suzhou Street in the Summer Palace?
   A. A modern shopping mall
   B. An ancient Chinese market street
   C. A futuristic city

## Reading 阅读下面的文章

The Summer Palace in Beijing is a very famous place and it's the biggest ancient **royal** garden in China. It's not just a park; it's full of history and beautiful stories.

The Summer Palace was first built around 1750 during the reign of Emperor Qianlong of the Qing Dynasty. Emperor Qianlong built it to celebrate his mother's birthday. Inside, there are lovely lakes, hills, and palaces, and each place has its own story.

The biggest **highlights** of the Summer Palace are Kunming Lake and the Long **Corridor**. Kunming Lake is a big man-made lake with a famous bridge called the Seventeen-Arch Bridge. This stone bridge is about 150 metres long and 8 metres wide, and it has more than 500 stone lions carved along its railings (栏杆).

The Long Corridor is a **walkway** that's about 728 metres long, covered in traditional Chinese paintings that **include landscapes**, flowers, birds, fish, insects, and **historical figures**. It's so pretty! Walking there, you can see the views of the lake and it feels like you're walking inside a beautiful painting.

**Besides** these, the Summer Palace has many other beautiful buildings and gardens. For example, the Tower of Buddhist Incense (佛香阁) is on a little hill. You can climb to the top and see the whole view of the Summer Palace. There's also a place called Suzhou Street that looks like an ancient

Chinese market street. You can see lots of traditional shops and small bridges over water, giving you a feel of old Chinese market **vibes**.

The Summer Palace isn't just a **relaxing** place; it's an important part of China's cultural heritage. In 1998, the Summer Palace was named a World Heritage Site by UNESCO, which shows its important place and value in the world.

## Vocabulary and phrases 词汇和短语

royal ['rɔɪəl] 形 皇家的
corridor ['kɒrɪdɔː(r)] 名 走廊
include [ɪn'kluːd] 动 包括
historical [hɪ'stɒrɪkl] 形 历史的
besides [bɪ'saɪdz] 副 此外
relaxing [rɪ'læksɪŋ] 形 轻松的

highlight ['haɪlaɪt] 名 亮点；重点
walkway ['wɔːkweɪ] 名 人行道
landscape ['lændskeɪp] 名 风景
figure ['fɪɡə(r)] 名 人物
vibe [vaɪb] 名 氛围

## Practice 请选择合适的词填在下方的横线上

royal    Corridor    include    historical    relaxing

1. The paintings also depict _____ figures.
2. The Summer Palace isn't just a _____ place; it's an important part of China's cultural heritage.
3. These paintings _____ landscapes, flowers, and birds.
4. The Long _____ is covered in traditional Chinese paintings.
5. The Summer Palace is the biggest ancient _____ garden in China.

## Talking practice 情景对话模拟练习

苏珊正在询问李明关于颐和园的一些情况,你能跟着一起练习这段对话吗?

Li Ming, can you tell me when the Summer Palace was first built?
李明,你能告诉我颐和园是什么时候建造的吗?

Susan苏珊

Li Ming李明

It was first built around 1750 during the reign of Emperor Qianlong.
它最初建于1750年左右,乾隆皇帝在位时期。

What was the reason behind its construction?
建造它的原因是什么?

Susan苏珊

Li Ming李明

Well, Emperor Qianlong built it to celebrate his mother's birthday.
乾隆皇帝为了庆祝他母亲的生日而建造了它。

What are some of the main attractions in the Summer Palace?
颐和园有哪些主要景点?

Susan苏珊

Li Ming李明

The Kunming Lake and the Long Corridor are the biggest highlights.
昆明湖和长廊是最大的亮点。

What's special about the Long Corridor?
长廊有什么特别之处?

Susan苏珊

Li Ming李明

It's a long walkway covered with traditional Chinese paintings, offering beautiful views of the lake.
它是一个长走道,覆盖着传统的中国画,可以看到湖的美丽景观。

## Funny facts  关于颐和园的有趣事实和短语

昆明湖的由来：昆明湖是颐和园的主体水域，其实是人工湖。它的建造灵感来自西湖，乾隆帝希望在北京重现西湖的美景。

设计理念：颐和园的设计充分展示了中国园林艺术的精髓，园中山水布局、建筑位置都讲究"借景"，自然地形与远处的景色相得益彰。

颐和园的石舫：石舫位于昆明湖西岸，是一座大型石结构的船形建筑，其设计独特，既象征稳固又富有装饰性。

Longevity Hill – 万寿山
Marble Boat – 石舫
Hall of Benevolence and Longevity – 仁寿殿
Hall of Jade Ripples – 玉澜堂

Hall of Joyful Longevity – 乐寿堂
bronze bull – 铜牛
Harmonious Pleasures Garden – 谐趣园
Great Stage – 大戏楼

## Writing practice  写作小练习

**根据我们这一节所学到的内容，写出下面句子的英文。**

1. 北京的颐和园是一个著名的皇家园林。

2. 昆明湖和长廊是颐和园里非常有名的景点。

3. 走在长廊上，你能看到很多精彩的中国画和美丽的湖景。

## Reference translation 参考译文

北京的颐和园是一座闻名遐迩的地方,它是中国最大的古代皇家园林。颐和园不仅是一个公园,它还是一个充满历史和美丽故事的地方。

颐和园始建于大约1750年,正值清朝乾隆皇帝在位时期。当时,乾隆皇帝为了庆祝他的母亲的生日,特地建了这个园林。颐和园内有湖泊、山石和宫殿,每一处都蕴含着独特的故事。

颐和园的最大亮点是昆明湖和长廊。昆明湖是一个大的人工湖,湖上还有一个很有名的十七孔桥。这座石桥全长约150米,宽8米,栏杆上雕有石狮500多只。

长廊是一条绵延约728米的步道,上面画满了中国传统的绘画,内容包括山水风景、花鸟鱼虫、人物典故等,非常漂亮!漫步其间,仿佛置身于一幅幅精美的画卷之中,湖光山色尽收眼底。

除了这些,颐和园还有很多美丽的建筑和花园。比如佛香阁,它位于一个小山丘上,登高望远,可将颐和园全景尽收眼底。还有一个名叫苏州街的地方,那里模仿了中国古代的商业街,你可以看到很多传统的店铺和小桥流水,感受古代中国的市场气氛。

颐和园不仅是一个让人放松的好地方,更是中国文化遗产的重要组成部分。1998年,颐和园被联合国教科文组织列为世界文化遗产,彰显了其在世界范围内的重要地位和价值。

# The Yungang Grottoes
## 云冈石窟：巧夺天工的雕刻艺术

**Listening & practice** 听英文原声，完成练习

▶扫码听音频◀

1. Where are the Yungang Grottoes located?
   A. Beijing
   B. Shanghai
   C. Datong, Shanxi Province

2. How long ago were the Yungang Grottoes started?
   A. About 1,500 years ago
   B. About 2,000 years ago
   C. About 500 years ago

3. What was the main reason for building the Yungang Grottoes?
   A. For entertainment
   B. To bring peace and happiness
   C. For business

4. How tall is the biggest Buddha statue in the Yungang Grottoes?
   A. 17 metres tall
   B. 10 metres tall
   C. 5 metres tall

5. What are the caves at Yungang Grottoes made of?
   A. Gold
   B. Sandstone
   C. Wood

## Reading 阅读下面的文章

The Yungang Grottoes are a really special place in Datong City, in Shanxi Province, China. They're made up of old Buddhist caves and are one of China's four famous grottoes.

About 1,500 years ago, people started carving these caves. Emperors and nobles from the Northern Wei Dynasty built them, hoping the Buddha statues would bring peace to the country and happiness to people. They worked on these carvings for about 150 years to make what we see today.

There are 45 main caves at Yungang, with more than 50,000 Buddha statues inside. These statues are all different sizes. Some are just a few inches tall, and the biggest one is 17 metres tall—that's as tall as a building! The caves have paintings and sculptures that are very pretty and tell us about how people long ago lived and what they believed in.

Walking into the Yungang Grottoes is like walking into a big history book. Each cave is like a little room full of beautiful carvings on the walls and ceilings. These carvings tell stories about Buddha and show what everyday life was like back then.

The way the Yungang Grottoes are built is really cool. Most of the caves are carved into cliffs made of sandstone. Even though some caves are a bit worn out from the weather, they still look great and show how skilled the old craftsmen were.

It's also super interesting that some of the caves have designs from places far away, like ancient India and Central Asia, and even some styles from ancient Greece and Rome. This shows that long ago, China was talking and sharing with many other big civilizations around the world.

Because the Yungang Grottoes are so important for their history, art, and culture, they were named a key protected site in China in 1961 and became a World Heritage Site by UNESCO in 2001. The Yungang Grottoes are not just old places; they help us learn about ancient Chinese culture and art.

## Vocabulary and phrases 词汇和短语

province ['prɒvɪns] 名 省

northern ['nɔːðən] 形 北部的；北方的

sculpture ['skʌlptʃə(r)] 名 雕塑；雕刻

history ['hɪstri] 名 历史

interesting ['ɪntrəstɪŋ] 形 有趣的

grotto ['grɒtəʊ] 名 洞穴；岩穴

cave [keɪv] 名 洞窟；洞穴

believe [bɪ'liːv] 动 相信；认为

carve [kɑːv] 动 雕刻

learn about 短 了解；知道

## Practice 请选择合适的词填在下方的横线上

> Grottoes    Province    sculptures    interesting    learn about

1. There are many beautiful _____ and paintings that tell stories about Buddhism.

2. From these carvings, we can _____ the Buddhist beliefs and culture.

3. Visiting the Yungang _____ is like stepping into a magical world of history and art.

4. The vivid carvings inside the cave make it an _____ place to visit and explore.

5. Yungang Grottoes in Datong, Shanxi _____, are a world cultural heritage site.

## Talking practice 情景对话模拟练习

在云冈石窟前，一位游客正在和导游交流，你能够跟着练习这段对话吗？

Tourist游客

How old are the Yungang Grottoes?
云冈石窟有多久的历史了？

Guide导游

They were started about 1,500 years ago during the Northern Wei Dynasty.
它们开始于大约1,500年前的北魏时期。

Tourist游客

What was the purpose of creating these caves?
创建这些洞窟的目的是什么？

Guide导游

The emperors and nobles hoped the Buddha statues would bring peace to the country and happiness to people.
皇帝和贵族希望佛像能给国家带来和平，给人们带来幸福。

Tourist游客

How many Buddha statues are there in the caves?
洞窟里有多少佛像？

Guide导游

There are over 50,000 Buddha statues in 45 main caves.
有45个主要洞窟中超过50,000尊佛像。

Tourist游客

What's unique about the designs in the Yungang Grottoes?
云冈石窟的设计有什么独特之处？

Guide导游

The caves have styles from different parts of the world, showing how ancient China communicated with other cultures.
这些洞窟展示了来自世界各地的风格，显示了古代中国如何与其他文化交流。

## Funny facts 关于云冈石窟的有趣事实和短语

**四大名窟**：中国的四大名窟指的是位于甘肃敦煌的莫高石窟、山西大同的云冈石窟、河南洛阳的龙门石窟以及甘肃天水的麦积山石窟。

**著名石窟**：第五窟（也被称为大佛洞）是云冈石窟中最大也最著名的一个，其中北面的坐佛高达17米，雄伟壮观。

**文化意义**：云冈石窟不仅是佛教艺术的宝库，也是研究中国历史、宗教和社会变迁的重要资料。石窟中的壁画和雕塑展示了当时的服饰、乐器、建筑和日常生活场景。

**技术与创新**：云冈石窟的雕刻技术在当时是前所未有的，从粗糙的切割到精细的雕琢，每一个细节都精心制作，展示了高超的工艺水平。

Buddhist sculptures – 佛教雕塑
stone caves – 石窟
carved statues – 雕刻的塑像
religious art – 宗教艺术
cultural tourism – 文化旅游
artistic legacy – 艺术遗产

## Writing practice 写作小练习

**根据我们这一节所学到的内容，写出下面句子的英文。**

1. 云冈石窟是中国规模最大的古代石窟群之一。

2. 这座石窟吸引了来自世界各地的游客。

3. 每个洞窟都有其独特的风格，雕刻着众多的雕塑和壁画（murals）。

# Reference translation 参考译文

云冈石窟位于中国山西省大同市，是一个极为特别的地方。它由一群古老的佛教石窟组成，是中国四大石窟之一。

大约在1,500年前，云冈石窟的雕刻工作开始了。北魏的皇帝和贵族们建造了它们，他们希望通过修建这些佛像来保佑国家安定和人民幸福。石窟的雕刻持续了大约150年，最终形成了今天我们看到的规模。

云冈石窟内有45个主要石窟，藏有超过5万尊佛像。这些佛像大小不一，有的仅有几英寸高，而最大的则有17米高，与一座建筑相当！石窟中的壁画和雕塑不仅艺术价值很高，还为我们提供了大量关于古代人民生活和宗教信仰的信息。

走进云冈石窟，就像是走进了一本宏大的历史书。每一个洞窟都像是一个小房间，洞窟的墙壁和天花板上都覆盖着精美的雕刻。这些雕刻描绘了佛教故事，也有很多展示日常生活场景的图案。

云冈石窟的建筑特色也非常独特。这些洞窟大多数挖在砂岩的山壁上。尽管有些石窟因天气原因有些磨损，但它们仍然展现出非凡的美丽，彰显了古代工匠的高超技艺。

同样超有趣的是，云冈石窟中的一些建筑也具有西方的样式，比如古印度、中亚艺术元素，也有古希腊、古罗马建筑造型等，这表明在很久以前，中国就已经与世界各地的其他伟大文明进行了交流和分享。

由于云冈石窟在历史、艺术和文化方面的重要性，它们在1961年被列为中国的国家重点文物保护单位，2001年更是被联合国教科文组织评为世界文化遗产。云冈石窟不仅是一处古迹，更帮助我们了解古代中国的文化和艺术。

# Fujian Tulou
## 福建土楼：独具特色的建筑艺术

**Listening & practice** 听英文原声，完成练习

▶扫码听音频◀

1. What province is Tulou in?
    A. Guangdong
    B. Fujian
    C. Sichuan

2. Why was Fujian Tulou originally built?
    A. To be used as schools
    B. To protect from enemies and natural disasters (自然灾害)
    C. To serve as hotels

3. What materials (材料) are used to build Fujian Tulou?
    A. Glass and steel
    B. Earth, bamboo, and wood
    C. Plastic and concrete

4. What is the shape of most Fujian Tulou?
    A. Round or square
    B. Triangular
    C. Hexagonal

5. What can you do in the courtyard (庭院) of a Fujian Tulou?
    A. Play sports
    B. Celebrate festivals
    C. Go swimming

## Reading 阅读下面的文章

Fujian Tulou are special traditional residences in Fujian Province, China. They are mostly found in the southern mountains of Fujian. They are not just buildings; but also show how smart and united the people of southern Fujian are.

The history of Tulou goes back to the Song and Yuan Dynasties. They were first built by the Hakka and Minnan people in Fujian to protect themselves from enemies and natural disasters. Most Tulous are round or square, and they are made from local materials like earth, bamboo, and wood, which makes them very strong. Each Tulou can house dozens or even hundreds of families, just like a mini "castle".

The architecture of Tulou is very noticeable because of their structure and shape. The round Tulous are called "round buildings", and the square ones are called "square buildings". Inside, the rooms are stacked up layer by layer, and from the outside, they look like a huge beehive (蜂窝). Each Tulou has a big courtyard where people gather and celebrate festivals, which helps bring family members closer together.

Tulou are more than just places to live; they also show how much local people care about their families and communities. The design of Tulou allows all family members to live closely together and take care of their home. This unique building also serves as a tool for defense, as residents (居民) can support each other inside the Tulou to fend off any outside threats.

Because of their unique cultural and architectural value, Fujian Tulou was listed as a World Heritage Site by UNESCO in 2008. This not only recognizes the art of Tulou building but also its historical and cultural significance.

Fujian Tulou is not only a pride of China but also attracts visitors from all over the world. I hope you also get a chance to visit these unique buildings one day, to see their special charm and learn about how people live there!

## Vocabulary and phrases 词汇和短语

traditional [trəˈdɪʃənl] 形 传统的

disaster [dɪˈzɑːstə(r)] 名 灾难

structure [ˈstrʌktʃə(r)] 名 结构；构造

building [ˈbɪldɪŋ] 名 建筑物

recognize [ˈrekəgnaɪz] 动 认可；承认

pride [praɪd] 名 骄傲；自豪

mountain [ˈmaʊntən] 名 山；山脉

square [skweə(r)] 形 正方形的

stack [stæk] 动 堆积；堆放

support [səˈpɔːt] 动 支持；支撑

cultural [ˈkʌltʃərəl] 形 文化的

live [lɪv] 动 居住；生活

## Practice 请选择合适的词填在下方的横线上

traditional    square    buildings    live    recognized

1. Fujian Tulou are special _____ in Fujian province.
2. They are made of earth, wood, and stone, and have round or _____ shapes.
3. They tell us about the lives and traditions of the people who _____ there.
4. Tulou have been _____ by UNESCO as a World Heritage Site.
5. These ancient architectures blend _____ culture and modern life.

## Talking practice 情景对话模拟练习

安娜和李凯是大学同学,他们正在谈论福建土楼,你也跟着练习这段对话吧!

Li Kai, what exactly is a Fujian Tulou?
李凯,福建土楼究竟是什么?

Anna 安娜

Li Kai 李凯

Tulou are large, multi-family residences in Fujian, China, built with local materials like earth and bamboo.
土楼是中国福建的大型多家庭住宅,使用当地材料如土和竹子建造。

Why were they originally built?
它们最初是为什么建造的?

Anna 安娜

Li Kai 李凯

They were built by the Hakka and Minnan people to protect themselves from enemies and natural disasters.
它们由客家和闽南人建造,以保护自己免受敌人和自然灾害的侵害。

What's special about their shape?
它们的形状有什么特别之处?

Anna 安娜

Li Kai 李凯

Most are either round or square, which makes them look like giant beehives or castles.
大多数土楼是圆形或方形的,看起来像巨大的蜂巢或城堡。

Do they still use these buildings today?
他们今天还使用这些建筑吗?

Anna 安娜

Li Kai 李凯

Yes, people still live in them, and they attract tourists from all over the world.
是的,人们仍然住在其中,它们吸引了来自世界各地的游客。

## Funny facts  关于福建土楼的有趣事实和短语

**结构坚固**：福建土楼墙体多用黄土、石块和竹片混合材料筑成，厚度可达数米，非常坚固，这种结构使得土楼具有很好的抗地震和防火性能。

**形状多样**：尽管福建土楼多为圆形或方形，但还有半圆形、五角形、交椅形等多种形态，每种形态都有其独特的文化和历史背景。

**建筑功能与文化**：土楼不仅是居住的地方，还是家族文化传承的中心。许多土楼内部装饰有精美的木雕和石雕，这些装饰往往含有富有象征意义的图案，如祥龙、凤凰等，象征着吉祥和繁荣。

**Hakka** – 客家
**Mazu** – 妈祖
**communal living** – 集体生活

**protective structure** – 防护结构
**wooden beams** – 木梁

## Writing practice  写作小练习

根据我们这一节所学到的内容，写出下面句子的英文。

1. 福建土楼是福建特有的传统建筑。

2. 厚实的墙壁能够抵御强风和暴雨，保护居民的安全。

3. 这些建筑不仅是艺术的杰作，也是当地居民生活的一部分。

## Reference translation 参考译文

福建土楼是中国福建省的一种独特的传统民居,主要分布在福建南部的山区等地方,这些建筑不仅仅是房子,它们更是闽南人民智慧和团结的象征。

土楼的历史可以追溯到宋元时期,最早是由福建的客家人和闽南人为了防御外敌侵扰和自然灾害而建造的。土楼大多是圆形或者方形的,用当地的土、竹子和木头等材料建成,非常坚固。每座土楼可以容纳几十户甚至上百户人家,感觉就像是一个小型的"城堡"。

土楼的建筑特色非常明显,最引人注目的是它们的结构和形状。圆形的土楼称为"围楼",方形的则称为"方楼",里面的房间一层层叠起,从外观看起来就像是一个巨大的蜂窝。每座土楼都有一个大院子,人们在这里聚会、庆祝节日,增强了家族成员之间的联系。

土楼不仅仅是一个居住的地方,它也反映了当地人对家庭和社区的重视。土楼的设计让所有的家庭成员都能紧密地生活在一起,共同维护他们的家园。这种独特的建筑也使得土楼成为了一个防御工具,居民可以在土楼内部互相支持,抵御任何外来的威胁。

因为其独特的文化和建筑价值,福建土楼在2008年被联合国教科文组织列为世界文化遗产。这不仅是对土楼建筑艺术的认可,也是对其历史和文化意义的肯定。

福建土楼不仅是中国的骄傲,也吸引了世界各地的游客前来参观。希望将来你也有机会亲自去看看这些独特的建筑,体验一下它们独特的魅力和那里人们的生活方式!

# Suzhou Classical Gardens
苏州古典园林：东方园林的精致之美

**Listening & practice** 听英文原声，完成练习

▶扫码听音频◀

1. How long ago did people start making gardens in Suzhou?
   A. 100 years ago
   B. 1,000 years ago
   C. Over 2,000 years ago

2. What did the rich people and retired officials in Suzhou use their gardens for?
   A. Sports
   B. Relaxation and to show their love for beauty
   C. Farming

3. What are some of the features found in Suzhou gardens?
   A. Skyscrapers and highways
   B. Mountains, ponds, and pavilions
   C. Shopping malls and cinemas

4. Which garden in Suzhou is the biggest?
   A. The Humble Administrator's Garden (拙政园)
   B. The Master of Nets Garden (网师园)
   C. The Lion Grove Garden (狮子林)

5. What is special about the windows in Suzhou gardens?
   A. They can change colours.
   B. They look nice and frame views like pictures.
   C. They open automatically.

## Reading 阅读下面的文章

Suzhou classical **gardens** are very pretty and special. They are not just **regular** gardens, they are like beautiful pictures made from **nature**.

A long, long time ago, over 2,000 years back in the Spring and Autumn Period, people started making these gardens. By the time of the Ming and Qing Dynasties, lots of rich people and **retired** officials loved to build their own gardens. These gardens were places for fun and also showed how much they loved beautiful things.

Suzhou gardens are built in a cool way. They use mountains, buildings, and **plants** to make a place where everything looks nice together. Some mountains in the gardens are real, but many are made from stones stacked up; the water areas are made with ponds and little rivers that go well with the **pavilions** and curvy bridges around them.

Every bridge and path in the gardens means something special, and every part is made to make people feel happy and calm.

Some of the most famous gardens in Suzhou are the Humble Administrator's Garden (拙政园), Lingering Garden (留园), Lion Grove Garden (狮子林), and the Master of Nets Garden (网师园). The Humble Administrator's Garden is the biggest and has lovely water scenes and **twisty** paths. The Lingering Garden is known for its pretty buildings and big water areas. The Lion Grove is famous for its cool rocky hills and **mysterious** paths, and the Master of Nets Garden is known for being very pretty and fancy.

Suzhou gardens also have lots of special windows that look nice and are useful for seeing different parts of the garden, like pictures in a painting.

Whether it's hot in summer, cold in winter, or during the pretty spring and fall, Suzhou gardens are perfect places to **enjoy** nature. This design shows how good ancient Chinese people were at making gardens, and it shows how they liked to live **peacefully** with nature.

In 1997, these gardens in Suzhou were named a World Heritage Site by UNESCO. This was to show how important and special Suzhou gardens are and to **celebrate** the old Chinese garden culture.

## Vocabulary and phrases 词汇和短语

garden ['gɑːdn] 名 公园；园子

nature ['neɪtʃə(r)] 名 自然；大自然

plant [plɑːnt] 名 植物

twisty ['twɪsti] 形 弯弯曲曲的；曲折的

enjoy [ɪn'dʒɔɪ] 动 欣赏；享受

celebrate ['selɪbreɪt] 动 赞美；庆祝

regular ['regjələ(r)] 形 普通的；平常的

retired [rɪ'taɪəd] 形 退休的

pavilion [pə'vɪliən] 名 楼阁

mysterious [mɪ'stɪəriəs] 形 神秘的；不可思议的

peacefully ['piːsfəli] 副 平静地；平和地

## Practice 请选择合适的词填在下方的横线上

> gardens    plants    regular    twisty    enjoy

1. Suzhou gardens are not just _____ gardens, but rather like a painting.

2. Suzhou, a beautiful city in China, is famous for its _____.

3. They wanted to create a place where they could relax and _____ nature.

4. You can walk along the _____ paths, listen to the sound of running water and watching the fish swimming in the ponds.

5. Many _____ in Suzhou Gardens have symbolic meanings, just like bamboo representing strength and integrity.

## Talking practice 情景对话模拟练习

来自国外的杰克第一次到访苏州园林,他和当地的导游陈芳展开了一段对话。

Jack杰克

**How old are Suzhou Gardens?**
苏州的园林有多久的历史了?

Chen Fang陈芳

**They date back over 2,000 years, starting in the Spring and Autumn Period.**
它们的历史可以追溯到2,000多年前的春秋时期。

Jack杰克

**Why were these gardens built?**
这些园林为什么会建造呢?

Chen Fang陈芳

**Rich people and retired officials built them as places for enjoyment and to express their love for beauty.**
富人和退休官员建造这些园林,作为享乐之地,并表达他们对美的热爱。

Jack杰克

**What makes these gardens so special in design?**
这些园林的设计有什么特别之处吗?

Chen Fang陈芳

**They use rocks, water, and plants to make everything look pretty together.**
它们利用岩石、水和植物共同营造美丽的景观。

Jack杰克

**Can you name a few famous gardens here?**
你能说几个这里的著名园林吗?

Chen Fang陈芳

**Certainly! The Humble Administrator's Garden and the Lingering Garden are among the most renowned.**
当然可以!拙政园和留园是其中最著名的园林。

## Funny facts  关于苏州古典园林的有趣事实和短语

**园林数量和历史**：苏州现存的古典园林超过450处，其中一些最著名的园林如拙政园、留园、网师园和狮子林等都有数百年的历史，可以追溯到明朝和清朝时期。

**园林功能**：传统上，苏州园林不仅仅是私人住所的一部分，它们还具有社交、娱乐功能。园林经常用于家族聚会、朋友聚会和各种节日庆典。

**文学与艺术**：苏州园林不仅是休闲和聚会的场所，也是文人墨客创作诗文、绘画和书法的灵感来源。许多园林都有专门的书法和艺术作品，体现了园主的文化品位和个人修养。

Lingering Garden – 留园
Humble Administrator's Garden – 拙政园
Lion Grove Garden – 狮子林
Master of Nets Garden – 网师园
Pavilion of Surging Waves – 沧浪亭

Couple's Retreat Garden – 耦园
moon gate – 月亮门
rockery – 假山
lotus pond – 荷花池
yea house – 茶室

## Writing practice  写作小练习

根据我们这一节所学到的内容，写出下面句子的英文。

1. 漫步在苏州园林中，你可以感受到浓厚的中国古典文化氛围。

2. 苏州园林中的假山、流水、石桥和楼阁构成一幅美丽画卷。

3. 苏州园林以其精美的设计和独特的风格吸引了无数游客。

## Reference translation 参考译文

苏州古典园林非常精美和特别。它们不仅是普通的花园,更像是大自然精心绘制的绝美画卷。

很久很久以前,距今已有两千余年的春秋时代,人们便已开始着手打造这些园林。及至明清,众多富商巨贾与退隐官员更是热衷于营建自己的园林府邸。这些园林,既是游乐之地,也彰显了他们对美好事物的无限热爱。

苏州园林的构建别具一格。它们巧妙运用山峦、建筑与植物,营造出一个和谐共生、美不胜收的天地。园中的山,既有真山,亦不乏以石堆砌而成的假山;水则以池塘、小溪为主,与周边的亭台楼阁、蜿蜒小桥相映成趣。

园中的每一座桥、每一条小径,都蕴含着特殊的意义,每一处细节都旨在让人心生愉悦、宁静致远。

其中,拙政园、留园、狮子林和网师园是最著名的几个苏州园林。拙政园是苏州最大的园林,以其秀美的水景与曲折的小径而著称。留园则以其精美的建筑和广阔的水面闻名。狮子林以奇特的石山和曲径通幽的路径闻名,而网师园则以其精巧和雅致著称。

此外,苏州园林还设有众多独特的窗棂,它们不仅美观大方,更能让游人透过窗棂,窥见园林的别样景致,仿佛置身于一幅幅精美的画卷之中。

无论是炎炎夏日、凛冽寒冬,还是明媚春光、金黄秋色,苏州园林都是人们亲近自然的绝佳去处。这种设计展示了中国古代园林艺术的精湛技艺,也反映了中国文化中人与自然和谐相处的追求。

1997年,苏州的这些园林被联合国教科文组织列为世界文化遗产,这既彰显了苏州园林的重要与独特,又是对古老中国园林文化的一次颂扬。

# Pingyao Ancient City
## 平遥古城：跨越千年的城市

**Listening & practice**  听英文原声，完成练习

▶扫码听音频◀

1. Where is Pingyao Ancient City located?
   A. In the middle of Shanxi Province, China
   B. In the southern part of Shandong Province, China
   C. On the eastern coast of China

2. What is special about the walls around Pingyao City?
   A. They have 72 towers.
   B. They are 72 metres high.
   C. They have 7 gates.

3. What do the 72 towers on the city wall stand for?
   A. The gates of the city
   B. The wise students of Confucius (孔子)
   C. Different cities

4. What was Rishengchang in Pingyao?
   A. A temple
   B. A school
   C. One of China's first banks

5. Why is Pingyao also called "Turtle City"?
   A. Because it has many turtles
   B. Because the city design looks like a turtle
   C. Because turtles were discovered there

## Reading 阅读下面的文章

Pingyao Ancient City is in the middle of Shanxi Province in China. It is one of the best-preserved ancient Chinese cities. The city is very old, started during the Western Zhou Dynasty, which means it is over 2,800 years old! Pingyao is famous for its very old buildings and lots of cool history.

First, the walls around Pingyao Ancient City are super impressive and a big part of the city. They were rebuilt early in the Ming Dynasty and are about 6 kilometres long and 10 metres high. There are six gates in the wall, each with a special design to keep the city safe. The wall also has 72 towers, which represent the 72 wise students of Confucius (孔子), showing how much people here respected his teachings.

The streets inside Pingyao are straight and wide, and the buildings from the Ming and Qing Dynasties along the streets are well-kept. Most buildings are made with grey bricks and tiles, and they look very old-fashioned with big wooden doors and beautifully carved windows. The most famous buildings include the City God Temple and the Rishengchang Bank, and each place has its own interesting stories.

Pingyao was not just a place with old buildings; it also helps us learn about ancient business. For example, Rishengchang Draft Bank was one of China's first banks, showing old money and tools for trading. Back in the Ming and Qing Dynasties, this place was full of shops and was very busy.

It's fun to know that the whole design of Pingyao Ancient City looks like an ancient turtle, so it's also called "Turtle City". In ancient Chinese culture, turtles mean good luck and long life.

In 1997, UNESCO put Pingyao Ancient City on the World Heritage List. This was to show that Pingyao is really important for its history and culture, and it lets even more people learn about this thousand-year-old city.

## Vocabulary and phrases 词汇和短语

middle ['mɪdl] 形 中间的；中央的

impressive [ɪm'presɪv] 形 令人叹为观止的

straight [streɪt] 形 直的

turtle ['tɜːtl] 名 龟；海龟

bank [bæŋk] 名 银行

famous ['feɪməs] 形 著名的；有名的

rebuild [ˌriː'bɪld] 动 重建；恢复

brick [brɪk] 名 砖；砖块

for example 短 例如；举例来说

mean [miːn] 动 意味着；意指

## Practice 请选择合适的词填在下方的横线上

> impressive    rebuilt    banks    straight    For example

1. Three of these towers have been _____, preserving a piece of the city's historical charm.

2. The South Street is such a _____ road, which serves as the central axis of the city.

3. Rishengchang Draft Bank became one of the largest _____ in northern China during its heyday (全盛期).

4. Pingyao Ancient City is an _____ testament to Chinese history and culture.

5. The surrounding attractions are also well worth a visit. _____, Qiao's Grand Courtyard is also a famous scenic spot.

## Talking practice 情景对话模拟练习

瑞秋对中国的文化非常感兴趣,她向好朋友陈玲询问起平遥古城的知识,请你跟着一起来练习这段对话吧。

**How old is Pingyao Ancient City?**
平遥古城有多久的历史了?

Rachel瑞秋

Chen Ling陈玲

**It's over 2,800 years old, starting from the Western Zhou Dynasty.**
它的历史超过2,800年,始于西周时期。

**What's special about the city walls?**
城墙有什么特别之处?

Rachel瑞秋

Chen Ling陈玲

**The walls are 6 kilometres long and have 72 watchtowers, each representing one of Confucius' wise students.**
城墙长6公里,有72座瞭望塔,每一座都代表孔子的一位贤徒。

**Are there any famous buildings in Pingyao?**
平遥有哪些著名的建筑?

Rachel瑞秋

Chen Ling陈玲

**Yes, the City God Temple and the Rishengchang Draft Bank are very famous. Each has its own unique story.**
有的,城隍庙和日升昌银行非常有名。每个地方都有它独特的故事。

**What did Rishengchang do?**
日升昌是做什么的?

Rachel瑞秋

Chen Ling陈玲

**It was one of China's first banks and was crucial for trade during the Ming and Qing Dynasties.**
它是中国最早的银行之一,在明清时期对贸易非常重要。

## Funny facts  关于平遥古城的有趣事实和短语

**防御系统**：平遥古城的城墙非常壮观，全长超过6公里，平均高度约10米，城墙最宽的地方可达12米左右，并拥有六个城门，城门上各有一个独特的角楼。这些城墙至今仍然屹立不倒，是中国古代城市防御系统的一个生动见证。

**金融历史**：平遥在清朝时期是中国北方的金融中心之一。著名的日升昌票号就设在这里，是中国最早的银行之一，其历史的重要性可与意大利的梅迪奇家族相媲美。

**影视拍摄地**：平遥古城因其保存完好的古建筑和古街道，而成为多部电影和电视剧的拍摄地。这些作品通过展示平遥的古典美，帮助世界了解中国丰富的历史和文化。

**Rishengchang Draft Bank** – 日升昌票号
**Confucious' Temple** – 文庙
**City God Temple** – 城隍庙

**Nine Dragon Screen** – 九龙壁
**Ming and Qing Street** – 明清街
**Shanxi Courtyard Houses** – 山西四合院

## Writing practice  写作小练习

根据我们这一节所学到的内容，写出下面句子的英文。

1. 平遥古城是中国保存最完好的古城之一。

   _____

2. 中国最早的银行日升昌就在平遥古城。

   _____

3. 平遥古城是参考古代神龟的图案所设计，所以也被称为"龟城"。

   _____

# Reference translation 参考译文

平遥古城位于中国山西省中部,是中国保存最完整的一座古城之一。这座城市的历史非常悠久,始建于西周时期,距今已有超过2,800年的历史。平遥古城以其古朴的建筑与丰富的历史底蕴而闻名遐迩。

首先来说,平遥古城的城墙非常壮观,是这座城市的一大特色。城墙重建于明朝初年,全长约6公里,城墙高度10米,有六个城门,每个城门都有独特的防御设计。城墙上还建有72个城楼,寓意着孔子门下七十二贤士,彰显了古城人民对儒家文化的崇敬与传承。

平遥古城内的街道平直宽敞,街道两旁是许多保存完好的明清时期的建筑。这些建筑大多用青砖灰瓦建成,风格古朴,有着高大的木门和精美的砖雕窗户。最有名的建筑包括城隍庙、日升昌票号等,每一处都承载着独特的历史故事。

平遥古城不仅仅是一座拥有众多古迹的古城,它也可以帮助我们充分了解古代商业。比如,日升昌票号是中国最早的银行之一,展示了古代的货币和交易工具。在明清时期,这里商铺林立,非常繁荣。

有趣的是,整个平遥古城的设计宛如一只巨大的古龟,因此又有"龟城"之称。在中国的古代文化中,龟寓意着吉祥长寿。

1997年,平遥古城被联合国教科文组织列入世界文化遗产名录,这一殊荣不仅彰显了平遥古城在历史与文化方面的重要地位,也让更多的人有机会了解这座拥有千年历史的古城。

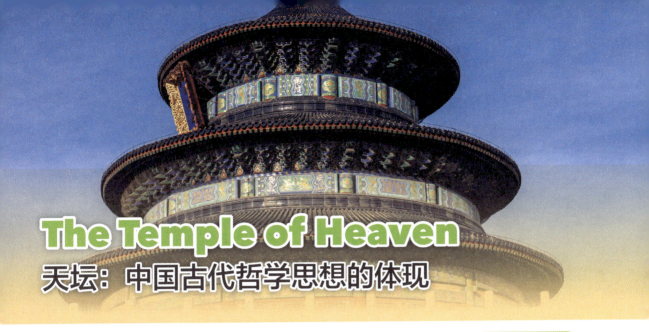

# The Temple of Heaven
天坛：中国古代哲学思想的体现

## Listening & practice 听英文原声，完成练习

扫码听音频

1. Which dynasty started the construction (建造) of the Temple of Heaven?
    A. Ming Dynasty
    B. Qing Dynasty
    C. Han Dynasty

2. What did the emperor pray for at the Hall of Prayer for Good Harvests (祈年殿)?
    A. Good weather
    B. Good crops and peace
    C. More land

3. What is special about the Circular Mound Altar (圜丘)?
    A. It's used every Summer Solstice.
    B. It's where the emperor held winter ceremonies.
    C. It's a place for daily prayers.

4. What does the blue colour on the buildings at the Temple of Heaven represent?
    A. The earth
    B. The sky
    C. Good luck

**5.** **What can you do at the Echo Wall (回音壁) in the Temple of Heaven?**
   A. See paintings
   B. Buy food
   C. Hear your echo

## Reading 阅读下面的文章

The Temple of Heaven in Beijing is a very special place. It's a famous symbol of Beijing and very important for Chinese culture. It was built over 600 years ago during the Ming Dynasty. Back then, emperors would go there to pray for good harvests.

The Temple of Heaven is really big — it's as big as more than 300 soccer fields! It has lots of trees and old buildings. Walking there is like traveling back in time. The biggest and coolest buildings are the Hall of Prayer for Good Harvests (祈年殿) and the Circular Mound (圜丘).

The Hall of Prayer for Good Harvests is a huge round building with a blue roof Symbolizing the Heaven. This is where the emperor prayed to heaven, hoping for good crops and peace. The Circular Mound is a large, open round altar where the emperor did special ceremonies every winter solstice (冬至日) to ask for heaven's blessings.

The buildings at the Temple of Heaven are made to show harmony between the sky and the earth, which is an old idea that the sky is round and the earth is square. The buildings are also colourful: blue stands for the sky, red means importance and good luck, and yellow is the colour of royalty.

There's also a really cool spot called the "Echo Wall". It's a smooth, curved wall about 200 metres long. If you whisper at one end, you can hear your voice at the other end— isn't that amazing?

In 1998, the Temple of Heaven was named a World Heritage Site by UNESCO, which means it's recognized as a treasure all over the world. This is not just because it's old and looks cool, but also because it shows a lot about Chinese culture and spirit.

## Vocabulary and phrases 词汇和短语

heaven ['hevn] 名 天空；天堂

temple ['templ] 名 寺庙；神殿

roof [ruːf] 名 屋顶；顶

harmony ['hɑːməni] 名 和谐；协调

royalty ['rɔɪəlti] 名 皇家；皇族

amazing [ə'meɪzɪŋ] 形 令人惊异的

harvest ['hɑːvɪst] 名 收成；收获

soccer ['sɒkə(r)] 名 足球

ceremony ['serəməni] 名 仪式；典礼

stand for 短 代表；象征

whisper ['wɪspə(r)] 动 低声说；窃窃私语

all over the world 短 全世界

## Practice 请选择合适的词填在下方的横线上

| temple    harvests    roof    ceremony    all over the world |

1. It was built as a place for emperors to worship Heaven and pray for good _____.

2. The Temple of Heaven attracts millions of visitors from _____ every year.

3. The blue _____ of the Temple of Heaven is a symbol of the sky and heaven.

4. This place was not only a _____; it is also a place of natural beauty.

5. The most famous _____ at the Temple of Heaven is the Winter Solstice Ceremony.

## Talking practice 情景对话模拟练习

一位游客正在天坛里游览,热心的导演向他介绍了天坛的知识,让我们练习这段对话吧。

How old is the Temple of Heaven?
天坛有多久的历史了?

Tourist游客

Guide导游

It was built over 600 years ago during the Ming Dynasty.
它建于600多年前的明朝时期。

What was the main purpose of this temple?
这座寺庙的主要用途是什么?

Tourist游客

Guide导游

Emperors used to come here to pray for good harvests.
皇帝们过去常来这里祈求丰收。

Which are the main buildings here?
这里的主要建筑有哪些?

Tourist游客

Guide导游

The Hall of Prayer for Good Harvests and the Circular Mound Altar are the most famous buildings at the Temple of Heaven.
祈年殿和圜丘是天坛里面最著名的建筑。

What's special about the Echo Wall?
回音壁有什么特别之处?

Tourist游客

天坛：中国古代哲学思想的体现　059

Guide导游

If someone whispers at one end, you can hear his voice at the other end of the wall.
如果有人在一端低语，你可以在墙的另一端听到他的声音。

Wow, that's amazing!
哇，这也太棒了！

Tourist游客

## Funny facts　关于天坛的有趣事实和短语

**符号和象征**：整个天坛的布局和每一个建筑的构成都充满了象征意义。例如，方形的地基代表地，圆形的建筑代表天，反映了古代中国"天圆地方"的宇宙观。

**九的运用**：圜丘的石阶、各层台面石和石栏板的数量，均采用"九"和"九"的倍数，以应"九重天"。通过对"九"的反复运用，以强调天的至高无上地位。

**祭天习俗**：一般情况下，在每次祭祀前，皇帝需提前三天到天坛内的斋宫斋戒，不吃肉、不饮酒、清正洁身，以表示对天的敬诚。

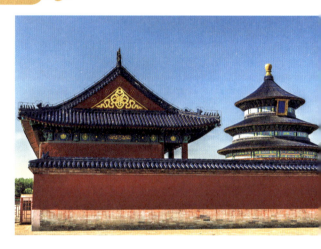

| Imperial Vault of Heaven – 皇穹宇 | Seven-Star Stones – 七星石 |
| Heavenly Centre Stone – 天心石 | North Heavenly Gate – 北天门 |
| Danbi Bridge – 丹陛桥 | Fasting Palace – 斋宫 |

## Writing practice　写作小练习

根据我们这一节所学到的内容，写出下面句子的英文。

1. 天坛是北京的地标之一，修建于明代。

_____

2. 祈年殿是一个巨大的圆形建筑，它的屋顶是蓝色的，代表着天空。

3. 皇帝会在这里祈求丰收。

## Reference translation 参考译文

北京的天坛是一个非常特别的地方，它不仅是北京的标志性建筑，更是中华文化的瑰宝。它始建于六百多年前的明朝，那时，帝王们常至此祈求风调雨顺、五谷丰登。

天坛的面积很大，相当于300多个足球场大。天坛里面绿树成荫，古建林立，漫步其间，恍若穿越时空。天坛里的建筑中最引人注目的是祈年殿和圜丘。

祈年殿是一个巨大的圆形建筑，它的屋顶是蓝色的，看起来像是天空。这个大殿是皇帝用来祭祀天神，祈求五谷丰登，国家安定的地方。圜丘则是一个露天的巨大圆形平台，每到冬至日，皇帝会在这里举行祭天大礼，祈求神明的保佑。

天坛的建筑，无不彰显着天地和谐，整个天坛的设计都体现了"天圆地方"的古老思想。建筑所使用的色彩丰富，蓝色代表天空，红色寓意庄严和吉祥，而黄色则体现出皇家的尊贵。

此外，天坛还有一个非常有趣的地方叫作"回音壁"。回音壁是一面周长约200米的光滑的弧形围墙，如果你在墙壁一端轻声说话，声音可以沿着墙壁传到很远的另一端，神奇不神奇？

1998年，天坛被联合国教科文组织列为世界文化遗产，成为全世界认可的文化珍宝。这不仅因为它的历史悠久，建筑独特，更因为它深深地蕴含了中国的文化和精神。

# Part 2
# 中国的经典艺术

# Peking Opera
# 京剧：当之无愧的"国粹"

## Listening & practice  听英文原声，完成练习

▶扫码听音频◀

1. **When did Peking Opera begin?**
   A. During the Tang Dynasty
   B. During the Qing Dynasty
   C. During the Ming Dynasty

2. **What are "Dan" roles in Peking Opera?**
   A. Male characters
   B. Female characters
   C. Funny characters

3. **What does a red mask represent in Peking Opera?**
   A. The character is tricky
   B. The character is brave
   C. The character is funny

4. **Which instrument (乐器) is used in Peking Opera?**
   A. Guitar
   B. Violin
   C. Jinghu

5. **What kind of stories does Peking Opera tell?**
   A. Only myths
   B. Only modern stories
   C. Old tales, myths, and stories about regular people

## Reading  阅读下面的文章

Peking Opera is a very famous type of theatre in China. It has a long history and a special way of performing, and is known as a key part of Chinese culture.

It began during the Qing Dynasty when Emperor Qianlong was in power. Peking Opera started by mixing different local opera styles, mainly from Anhui, and later added parts from Han plays and Kunqu opera.

In Peking Opera, actors focus a lot on how they perform. They sing, speak, act, and even do martial arts to show what their characters feel and to tell the story.

There are different kinds of roles in Peking Opera: "Sheng" for male characters, "Dan" for female characters, "Jing" for males with painted faces, and "Chou" for funny characters. Each type of role has its own way of acting and special costumes.

The costumes and makeup in Peking Opera are really beautiful and colourful. The outfits, especially the headpieces and masks, tell us a lot about who the characters are. For example, red masks mean the character is brave, and white masks mean they are tricky.

The music in Peking Opera uses instruments like the jinghu, flutes, and drums. This music is very pretty and helps make the plays exciting. There are many different stories in Peking Opera, from old tales and myths to stories about regular people. These plays are fun to watch and teach us about good values.

Peking Opera is not just loved in China but all over the world. In 2010, it was even named an Intangible Cultural Heritage by UNESCO. This shows it's really important and helps share Chinese culture with the whole world.

## Vocabulary and phrases 词汇和短语

theatre [ˈθɪətə] 名 戏剧

style [staɪl] 名 风格；式样

character [ˈkærəktə(r)] 名 角色；人物

especially [ɪˈspeʃəli] 副 特别；尤其

tricky [ˈtrɪki] 形 狡猾的；足智多谋的

flute [fluːt] 名 笛子

mix [mɪks] 动 混合

focus [ˈfəʊkəs] 动 聚焦

costume [ˈkɒstjuːm] 名 服装；剧装

headpiece [ˈhedpiːs] 名 头饰

instrument [ˈɪnstrəmənt] 名 乐器

exciting [ɪkˈsaɪtɪŋ] 形 令人兴奋的；使人激动的

## Practice 请选择合适的词填在下方的横线上

> theatres    character    costumes    tricky    instrument

1. The jinghu is a bowed string _____ similar to the western violin.

2. The _____ worn by the actors are designed to reflect the personalities, statuses and emotions.

3. Peking Opera is a form of traditional Chinese _____.

4. Each _____ in Peking Opera has a unique story and contributes to the overall narrative (故事) of the play.

5. In Peking Opera, white masks generally represent _____ characters.

## Talking practice 情景对话模拟练习

初到北京的迈克想去看京剧演出,他和同学王成聊起了这门艺术,你能模拟这段对话吗?

I've heard Peking Opera is really unique. What makes it so special?
我听说京剧非常独特。它有什么特别之处吗?

Mike迈克

Wang Cheng王成

It combines singing, speaking, acting, and acrobatic fighting. The performances are very expressive.
它结合了唱、念、做和打。表演非常富有表现力。

Are there different roles in Peking Opera?
京剧里有不同的角色吗?

Mike迈克

Wang Cheng王成

Yes, there are. For example, "Sheng" are the male roles, "Dan" are the female roles, and "Jing" characters have painted faces.
有的,比如"生"是男性角色,"旦"是女性角色,"净"则是画着脸谱的角色。

What about the costumes? They look really colourful.
那服装呢?看起来非常丰富多彩。

Mike迈克

Wang Cheng王成

The costumes are elaborate, and each colour and design has a meaning. For example, red masks signify bravery.
剧服非常精致,每种颜色和设计都有其含义。例如,红色面具代表勇敢。

And the music in Peking Opera, what's that like?
京剧的音乐是怎样的?

Mike 迈克

Wang Cheng 王成

The music uses traditional instruments like the jinghu and drums to enhance the atmosphere. It's quite beautiful.
音乐使用京胡和鼓这样的传统乐器来增强氛围。非常美。

## Funny facts 关于京剧的有趣事实和短语

**经典剧目**：京剧拥有大量的传统剧目，如《白蛇传》《空城计》《贵妃醉酒》《苏三起解》等。这些剧目通常基于中国古代的历史故事、民间传说和文学作品。

**独特的乐器**：京剧的音乐主要由打击乐器和弦乐器组成，包括鼓、钹、京胡和二胡等，音乐强调表达情感和推动剧情发展。

**四大名旦**：在早期，京剧中的旦角（女性角色）通常都是由男性来扮演，并催生出梅兰芳、程砚秋、尚小云、荀慧生四位著名的演员，并称"四大名旦"。

**face painting** – 脸谱
**water sleeves** – 水袖
**acrobatic fighting** – 武打

**role types** – 行当
**aria** – 唱腔

## Writing practice 写作小练习

**根据我们这一节所学到的内容，写出下面句子的英文。**

1. 京剧是中国的文化瑰宝之一。

2. 京剧中的脸谱是用不同的颜色在脸上勾画出来的。

3. 京剧的角色可以分为生、旦、净、丑。

## Reference translation 参考译文

京剧是中国最著名的戏剧形式之一,它有着丰富的历史和独特的表演风格,被誉为中国文化的重要组成部分。

京剧的起源可以追溯到清朝乾隆年间,最初是由多种地方戏曲融合发展而来的,尤其是吸收了安徽戏的许多元素,后来又融合了一些来自汉剧和昆曲的特点。

京剧的表演非常讲究舞台表现,包括唱(歌唱)、念(念白)、做(表演)、打(武术)四个基本功,演员通过这些技艺来表达人物的情感和故事情节。

京剧中有不同的角色类型:"生"代表男性角色,"旦"代表女性角色,"净"代表画有脸谱的男性角色,"丑"代表滑稽角色。每种角色类型都有其独特的表演方式和特殊的戏服。

京剧的戏服和化妆非常美丽且色彩斑斓。服饰,特别是头饰和面具,能告诉我们很多关于角色身份的信息。例如,红色面具代表角色勇敢,而白色面具则代表角色狡猾。

京剧的音乐伴奏主要由京胡、笛子、锣鼓等乐器组成,音乐旋律悠扬,能很好地配合演员的表演增强戏剧的感染力。京剧的剧目广泛,包括历史故事、神话传说、民间故事等,这些故事不仅娱乐观众,也传递了许多传统美德。

京剧不仅在中国有极高的地位,还受到了世界各地文化爱好者的喜爱和尊重。2010年,京剧被列入联合国教科文组织非物质文化遗产名录。这表明京剧确实非常重要,有助于向全世界传播中国文化。

# Chinese Painting
## 国画：独特的东方韵味

**Listening & practice** 听英文原声，完成练习

▶扫码听音频◀

1. What do Chinese painters use to make their paintings?
   A. Pencils and paper
   B. Brushes, ink, and rice paper or silk
   C. Crayons and cardboard

2. During which dynasties did Chinese painting become very popular?
   A. Tang and Song Dynasties
   B. Ming and Qing Dynasties
   C. Han and Yuan Dynasties

3. What do Chinese landscape paintings show?
   A. Oceans and ships
   B. Mountains and rivers
   C. Buildings and cars

4. What does the painting *Along the River During the Qingming Festival* (《清明上河图》) show?
   A. A quiet village
   B. A busy city during a festival
   C. A mountain scene

5. What do bamboo and pine trees mean in Chinese paintings?
   A. Strength
   B. Wealth
   C. Happiness

## Reading  阅读下面的文章

Chinese traditional painting is a very old and special type of art famous for its Eastern style and deep cultural meanings. These paintings are made with brushes, ink, and rice paper or silk. These tools help artists show their feelings about nature and life.

Chinese painting started a long time ago, especially during the Tang and Song Dynasties when it became really popular. Back then, painters worked hard to get better at their art and used it to share their ideas about poetry and life lessons. Famous people like Wang Wei and Su Dongpo were great at this kind of painting.

In Chinese paintings, you can see pictures of mountains, rivers, flowers, birds, and people. Landscape painting is very important and thought of as the heart of Chinese painting. These aren't just pictures of nature; they show the painters' deep feelings and dreams. Painting mountains and rivers carefully, they make art that feels like it takes you to another place that makes you feel calm and happy.

Flowers and birds are also important in these paintings. They come from old stories and thoughts about nature, showing colourful flowers and animals that make us love nature and dream of a lovely life. These paintings are full of colours and are pretty to look at, and they also make us think about big ideas.

There are many famous Chinese paintings. One special painting is *Along the River During the Qingming Festival* by Zhang Zeduan from the Northern Song Dynasty. It shows a busy city during a festival long ago with lots of people doing different things. It helps us see what life was like back then.

Chinese paintings are beautiful to look at and also share important messages through pictures and symbols. For example, bamboo and pine trees show strength and never giving **up**, plum blossoms mean **purity** and strength, and **cranes** are symbols of living a long and wise life.

## Vocabulary and phrases 词汇和短语

brush [brʌʃ] 名 毛笔；画笔

popular ['pɒpjələ(r)] 形 受欢迎的

poetry ['pəʊətri] 名 诗意；诗情

paint [peɪnt] 动 绘画

festival ['festɪvl] 名 节日

purity ['pjʊərəti] 名 纯净；纯洁

artist ['ɑːtɪst] 名 艺术家；画家

share [ʃeə(r)] 动 分享

thought [θɔːt] 名 思想；想法

lovely ['lʌvli] 形 美好的；快乐的

give up 短 放弃；抛弃

crane [kreɪn] 名 鹤

## Practice 请选择合适的词填在下方的横线上

artist's    painting    brush    given up    popular

1. The essence of Chinese paintings lies in its use of _____, ink, and colour on silk or paper.

2. It's also a reflection of the _____ thoughts, feelings, and understanding of the world.

3. Xu Beihong is a _____ Chinese painter, best-known for his paintings of horses.

4. Before _____, the painter must have a draft in his mind.

5. In the face of difficulties, Chinese painting artists have never _____.

## Talking practice 情景对话模拟练习

琳达对中国传统国画非常感兴趣，她向好朋友陈迪请教了一些问题，你也来跟着模拟这段对话吧。

Chen Di, can you tell me about Chinese traditional painting?
陈迪，你能给我介绍一下中国传统绘画吗？

Linda琳达

Chen Di陈迪

Sure, it's a very old art form using brushes, ink, and special paper or silk.
当然，这是一种运用毛笔、墨水和特制纸或丝绸的非常古老的艺术形式。

When did it become popular?
它是什么时候开始流行的？

Linda琳达

Chen Di陈迪

It became really popular during the Tang and Song Dynasties.
在唐朝和宋朝时期变得非常流行。

What do these paintings usually show?
这些画通常描绘什么内容？

Linda琳达

Chen Di陈迪

They often show mountains, rivers, flowers, birds, and people. Landscapes are very important.
它们经常描绘山水、花鸟和人物。山水画非常重要。

Why is landscape painting so important?
为什么山水画这么重要？

Linda琳达

Chen Di陈迪

It expresses the painter's deep feelings and dreams, making you feel calm and happy.
它们表达了画家深刻的情感和梦想，让人感到平静和快乐。

Are there any famous Chinese paintings?
有名的中国画有哪些呢?

Linda 琳达

Chen Di 陈迪

Yes, one famous painting is *Along the River During the Qingming Festival* by Zhang Zeduan, showing a busy city during a festival.
有,一幅著名的画是张择端的《清明上河图》,描绘了节日期间繁忙的城市。

## Funny facts 关于国画的有趣事实和短语

**三大类**:中国国画主要分为山水画(描绘自然景观)、花鸟画(描绘花卉和鸟类)和人物画(描绘人类形象和生活场景)三种类型,每种类型都有其独特的技法和表达方式。

**四君子**:国画中有四种植物被称为"四君子",它们分别是梅、兰、竹、菊。这些植物象征着高尚的品格和精神。

**著名画家**:历史上著名的国画家包括唐代的吴道子、宋代的张择端、元代的黄公望、明代的徐渭、清代的石涛等,他们的作品对后世影响深远。

ink wash painting – 水墨画
rice paper – 宣纸
landscape painting – 山水画
flower-and-bird painting – 花鸟画
four gentlemen – 四君子
figure painting – 人物画
*Along the River During the Qingming Festival* –《清明上河图》

*Dwelling in the Fuchun Mountains* –《富春山居图》
*Early Spring* –《早春图》
*Five Oxen* –《五牛图》
*A Thousand Li of Rivers and Mountains* –《千里江山图》

## Writing practice 写作小练习

**根据我们这一节所学到的内容,写出下面句子的英文。**

1. 国画经常描绘山水、花鸟和人物。

2. 国画是用毛笔和墨汁在宣纸或丝绸上作画的。

_____

3. 不同时期的国画反映出了当时人们对自然、社会的看法。

_____

## Reference translation 参考译文

中国传统国画是一种非常古老和独特的艺术形式，它以其独特的东方韵味和深刻的文化内涵著称于世。国画主要使用毛笔、墨水，以及宣纸或丝绸，这些材料加在一起，让画家可以自由地表达自己对自然美和生活感受的理解。

国画的历史可以追溯到中国古代，尤其是在唐宋时期，国画艺术达到了一个高峰。那个时候的画家们不仅注重画技的提升，更加强调通过画来表达诗意和哲理，许多著名的文人墨客如王维、苏东坡都是出色的国画大师。

在国画中，你能看到山水、花鸟、人物等主题。其中山水画尤为重要，被视为国画的灵魂。山水画不仅仅是对自然景观的再现，更是画家内心情感和精神追求的反映。画家们通过对山川、水流的细腻描绘，创作出仿佛能带你到另一个地方的艺术作品，让你感到宁静和快乐。

花鸟画也是国画中的重要组成部分。它们来源于古老的故事和对自然的思考，展示了丰富多彩的花卉和动物，寄寓了人们对自然的热爱和对美好生活的向往。这些画作不仅色彩丰富，构图优美，更蕴含了深厚哲学思考。

著名的国画作品数不胜数，其中《清明上河图》是中国国画中的瑰宝，由北宋时期的画家张择端创作。它描绘了一个节日期间繁忙的城市景象，许多人正在做各种事情。它帮助我们了解当时的生活状况。

中国国画不仅在视觉上给人以美的享受，更通过绘画和象征来隐喻。例如，竹子和松树常被用来象征坚韧不拔的品格，梅花则象征高洁和坚强的生命力，而鹤则代表了长寿与智慧。

# Porcelain
瓷器：让世界感到精湛的技艺

## Listening & practice  听英文原声，完成练习

1. **When did people in China start making real porcelain?**
   A. 500 years ago
   B. Over 2,000 years ago
   C. 1,000 years ago

2. **What was porcelain first used for?**
   A. Making toys
   B. Everyday needs like bowls and plates
   C. Building houses

3. **What colour porcelain was advanced during the Ming and Qing Dynasties?**
   A. Red and yellow
   B. Blue and white
   C. Green and purple

4. **What do dragons on porcelain mean?**
   A. Love
   B. Friendship
   C. Power

5. **Where can you see ancient Chinese porcelain today?**
   A. In museums around the world
   B. In schools
   C. In shopping malls

## Reading 阅读下面的文章

Chinese **porcelain** is a treasure of the world's ceramic art, known for its beautiful **craftsmanship** and deep cultural meaning. People in China started making real porcelain over two thousand years ago, during the Eastern Han period.

At first, porcelain was made for everyday needs like bowls, plates, pots, and jars. Porcelain is **waterproof** and **durable**, making it great for storing liquids like wine and vinegar.

As porcelain-making techniques **improved** and people wanted prettier things, porcelain became finer and more artistic. Besides being used for everyday things, porcelain also started to be used for **decoration** and in ceremonies. It showed off a person's taste and social status. At parties and important social events, beautiful porcelain was a key way to show wealth and culture.

Porcelain-making reached a peak during the Song Dynasty. Back then, porcelain was hard, shiny, and came in many types like green, white, and black porcelain. By the Ming and Qing Dynasties, the making of blue and white porcelain was very advanced, and porcelain craftsmanship reached new heights.

The designs on porcelain often have deep meanings. For example, lotus flowers represent cleanliness and elegance, and dragons stand for power and majesty. The shape and decoration of the porcelain also reflected the beauty standards and social trends of the time. For example, Song Dynasty porcelain emphasized simplicity and nature, while Ming and Qing porcelain focused more on rich colours and elaborate decorations.

Chinese porcelain was not only important inside China but was also a popular item traded on the maritime Silk Road, showing off China's excellent craftsmanship and helping to exchange cultures between East and West.

Today, ancient Chinese porcelain is often seen as a national treasure and is displayed in museums around the world, attracting many visitors. Each piece of porcelain carries the wisdom and hard work of ancient Chinese artisans and is an important window into Chinese history and culture.

## Vocabulary and phrases 词汇和短语

porcelain ['pɔːsəlɪn] 名 瓷器；瓷

waterproof ['wɔːtəpruːf] 形 防水的；耐水的

improve [ɪm'pruːv] 动 改进；提高

elegance ['elɪɡəns] 名 高雅；优雅

excellent ['eksələnt] 形 杰出的；极好的

museum [mjuˈziːəm] 名 博物馆

craftsmanship ['krɑːftsmənʃɪp] 名 技术；技艺

durable ['djʊərəbl] 形 耐用的；持久的

decoration [ˌdekəˈreɪʃn] 名 装饰

emphasize ['emfəsaɪz] 动 强调

exchange [ɪksˈtʃeɪndʒ] 动 交换

wisdom ['wɪzdəm] 名 智慧；才智

**Practice** 请选择合适的词填在下方的横线上

porcelain    improving    exchange    excellent    museum

1. The porcelain craftsmanship has been constantly _____ over the centuries.

2. Walking into the _____, my eyes were drawn to the display of Chinese porcelains.

3. There are many different types of Chinese _____, each with its own special beauty.

4. I imagined how skilled the artisans must have been to create such _____ works of art.

5. Chinese porcelain helps to _____ economy and culture between China and the outside world.

## Talking practice 情景对话模拟练习

在博物馆里，一位游客正在和导游交流中国瓷器的知识，你也跟着一起来练习这段对话吧。

Why is Chinese porcelain so famous?
为什么中国瓷器这么有名？

Tourist 游客

Guide 导游

It's known for being very beautiful and special.
它以非常美丽和特别而闻名。

How long have people been making it?
人们制作瓷器有多久了？

Tourist 游客

Guide 导游

People have been making porcelain for over 2,000 years.
人们制作瓷器已经超过两千年了。

What did they use it for?
他们用瓷器做什么？

Tourist 游客

Guide 导游

They used it for bowls, plates, and jars because it's strong and waterproof.
他们用它来做碗、盘子和罐子，因为它坚固防水。

When did it become more beautiful and fancy?
瓷器什么时候变得更美丽和华丽了？

Tourist 游客

Guide 导游

During the Ming and Qing Dynasties, porcelain became very fine and artistic.
在明清时期，瓷器变得非常精细和有艺术性。

**What do the designs mean?**
图案有什么意思?

Tourist 游客

Guide 导游

**Designs like lotus flowers mean cleanliness, and dragons mean power.**
像莲花这样的图案意味着洁净,而龙则意味着力量。

## Funny facts  关于瓷器的有趣事实和短语

瓷器与"China": 在英语中,"China"既表示中国,也表示瓷器,这表明瓷器是中国文化的重要代表之一。

五大名窑: 宋代的五大名窑包括汝窑、官窑、哥窑、定窑和钧窑,这些窑口生产的瓷器因其独特的釉色和纹理而闻名。

瓷器与茶文化: 瓷器在中国茶文化中扮演重要角色,茶壶、茶杯等器具多以瓷器制成,其细腻的材质能很好地保持茶香。

| | |
|---|---|
| blue and white porcelain – 青花瓷 | imperial kiln – 官窑 |
| famille rose porcelain – 粉彩瓷 | enamelware – 珐琅彩 |
| doucai – 斗彩 | |

## Writing practice  写作小练习

**根据我们这一节所学到的内容,写出下面句子的英文。**

1. 中国瓷器有超过2,000多年的历史了。

   _____

2. 他们用它来做碗、盘子和罐子。

   _____

3. 你可以在世界很多的博物馆里看到中国的瓷器。

   _____

## Reference translation 参考译文

中国古代瓷器是世界陶瓷艺术的瑰宝,以其精美的工艺和深厚的文化内涵闻名于世。早在距今两千多年前的东汉时期,中国人就开始制作真正的瓷器了。

瓷器最初的用途主要是为了满足日常生活的需要,常见的瓷器如碗、盘、壶、罐等。由于瓷器具有防水、耐用的特性,很适合用来保存液体,如酒和醋。

随着瓷器技术的进步和人们对美好事物的追求,瓷器的制作逐渐变得更加精细和艺术化。除了基本的生活用途外,瓷器也开始承载更多的装饰和礼仪功能,成为展示个人品位和社会地位的重要方式。在宴会和重要的社交场合,精美的瓷器是展示主人财富和文化修养的重要工具。

宋代是瓷器制作的一个鼎盛时期。那时候的瓷器不仅质地坚硬,色泽光润、纹路细腻,而且种类繁多,有青瓷、白瓷、黑瓷等多种类型。到了明清,青花瓷的烧制技术已经十分成熟,清瓷器的制作达到了一个新的高度。

瓷器上的图案往往富含深意,如莲花代表清洁高雅,龙表示权力和威严。瓷器的形状和装饰也反映了当时的审美观和社会风尚。例如,宋代的瓷器强调简洁、自然,而明清时期的瓷器则更加注重色彩的丰富和装饰的华丽。

中国的瓷器不仅在国内受到重视,还远销海外,尤其是在海上丝绸之路上,中国瓷器是极受欢迎的商品。它不仅展示了中国的高超工艺,还促进了东西方文化的交流。

如今,中国古代瓷器常被视为国宝,在世界各地的博物馆里展出,吸引了无数游客的目光。每一件瓷器都承载了中国古代工匠的智慧和心血,是了解中国历史和文化的重要窗口。

# Tang and Song Poetry
## 唐诗宋词：中国传统的诗歌艺术

### Listening & practice  听英文原声，完成练习

▶扫码听音频◀

1. **What are Tang Poems known for?**
   A. Beautiful words and deep feelings
   B. Funny stories
   C. Science facts

2. **Who is called the "Immortal Poet" (诗仙)?**
   A. Du Fu
   B. Su Shi
   C. Li Bai

3. **What does Song Poetry focus on?**
   A. Stories
   B. Sound and feelings
   C. Colours

4. **Which poet was from the Song Dynasty?**
   A. Li Bai
   B. Du Fu
   C. Su Shi

5. **What does Tang Poems and Song Poetry help us learn about?**
   A. Maths and science
   B. History and culture
   C. Cooking

## Reading 阅读下面的文章

Tang poetry and Song poetry are treasures of Chinese literature. They are famous for their pretty words and deep feelings. These two kinds of poetry come from important times in Chinese history.

Tang poetry is from the Tang Dynasty, a very rich and happy period in China. Two of the most famous poets were Li Bai and Du Fu.

Li Bai wrote romantic poems and is called the "Poetic Genius". Du Fu cared a lot about people and their problems, earning him the title of "Poetic Sage". Tang Poems include many themes like the beauty of nature, personal feelings, and poems that talk about society.

Song poetry is from the Song Dynasty and are another kind of poetry. They are softer and focus more on how the words sound and the feelings they express.

Famous Song poets include Su Shi and Li Qingzhao. Their poems talk about their own feelings and also show what life was like back then. Su Shi's poems are strong and heartfelt, while Li Qingzhao's poems are gentle and touch on deep emotions.

Tang poetry and Song poetry are very loved in China and have touched people all over the world. Their translated versions have spread far and wide, letting people everywhere enjoy classical Chinese literature. These poems help us appreciate nature's beauty, understand life's ups and downs, and feel deep emotions. They help us learn about China's history and culture.

Reading Tang poetry and Song poetry not only teaches us beautiful words but also helps us **understand** the history and culture behind them. We can learn about the wisdom and talent of people from long ago.

## Vocabulary and phrases 词汇和短语

literature ['lɪtrətʃə(r)] 名 文学

theme [θiːm] 名 主题

express [ɪk'spres] 动 表达

version ['vɜːʃn] 名 版本；译本

appreciate [ə'priːʃieɪt] 动 欣赏

understand [ˌʌndə'stænd] 动 了解；理解

romantic [rəʊ'mæntɪk] 形 浪漫的

poem ['pəʊɪm] 名 诗

emotion [ɪ'məʊʃn] 名 情感；情绪

classical ['klæsɪkl] 形 古典的

ups and downs 短 起伏；盛衰

## Practice 请选择合适的词填在下方的横线上

version   poetry   romantic   appreciate   literature

1. Li Bai, also known as "Poetic Genius", was renowned for his _____ poems.

2. Song poetry is a unique and vibrant form of Chinese _____ that deserves to be explored.

3. Unlike Tang poetry, Song _____ tend to be more flexible in form and style.

4. They can also _____ the beauty of the Chinese language through poetry.

5. The translated _____ has spread far and wide.

## Talking practice 情景对话模拟练习

吉姆最近对唐诗非常感兴趣,他向同学李玲请教了一些唐诗的知识,请你一起练习这段对话吧。

Li Ling, can you tell me about Tang poetry?
李玲,你能给我讲讲唐诗吗?

Jim吉姆

Li Ling李玲

Of course! Tang poetry is from the Tang Dynasty, a very prosperous time in China.
当然可以!唐诗来自唐朝,那是中国非常繁荣的时期。

Who are some famous poets from that time?
那个时期有哪些著名的诗人?

Jim吉姆

Li Ling李玲

Two of the most famous poets are Li Bai and Du Fu.
最著名的两位诗人是李白和杜甫。

What are their poems about?
他们的诗歌是关于什么的?

Jim吉姆

Li Ling李玲

Li Bai's poems are romantic and he is called the 'Poetic Genius'. Du Fu's poems focus on people's lives and problems, earning him the title 'Poetic Sage'.
李白的诗很浪漫,他被称为"诗仙"。杜甫的诗关注人民的生活和问题,因此被称为"诗圣"。

What does Tang poetry usually talk about?
唐诗通常讲些什么呢?

Jim吉姆

Li Ling李玲

It talks about nature, feelings, and life in society.
它们讲自然、情感和社会生活。

## Funny facts  关于唐诗宋词的有趣事实和短语

**数量巨大**：唐代是中国古典诗歌的黄金时代，《全唐诗》里收录的作品就有近五万首，超过2000多位诗人。

**歌唱起源**：宋代是词的繁荣时期，词最初是一种配乐歌唱的形式，后来逐渐成为独立的文学体裁。

**婉约与豪放**：宋词有两大主要风格流派。婉约派以李清照、柳永为代表，词风细腻柔美；豪放派以苏轼、辛弃疾为代表，词风豪迈奔放。

---

*quatrain* – 绝句
*The Complete of Tang Poems* – 《全唐诗》
*romanticism* – 浪漫主义
*realism* – 现实主义
*Quiet Night Thoughts* – 《静夜思》
*Spring Dawn* – 《春晓》
*The Night Mooring by Maple Bridge* – 《枫桥夜泊》

*Yellow Crane Tower* – 《黄鹤楼》
*The Song of Everlasting Regret* – 《长恨歌》
*Prelude to Water Melody* – 《水调歌头》
*Butterfly Loves Flowers* – 《蝶恋花》

---

## Writing practice  写作小练习

**根据我们这一节所学到的内容，写出下面句子的英文。**

1. 李白是中国历史上最有名的诗人之一。

   _____

2. 迄今为止，许多唐诗仍旧广为流传。

   _____

3. 唐诗通常讲述自然、情感和社会生活。

   _____

# Reference translation 参考译文

唐诗宋词是中国文学史上的瑰宝。它们以其优美的语言和深刻的情感表达而闻名。这两种诗歌形式都源自中国历史上的重要时期。

唐诗源自唐朝,这是中国历史上一个非常富饶和欢乐的时代。其中最有名的两位诗人是李白和杜甫。

李白的诗歌带有很强的浪漫色彩,被誉为"诗仙",而杜甫则因其深刻的社会关怀和对人民苦难的同情被称为"诗圣"。唐诗的主题广泛,包括描写大自然的美、表达个人情感,以及反映社会现实。

宋词则是宋朝的诗歌形式,宋词在表达方式上更加细腻柔和,更注重声音的韵律和情感的层次。

宋词的代表人物有苏轼和李清照。他们的作品不仅表达了个人的情感,还反映了当时社会的风貌和人们的生活状态。苏轼的词作激昂豪放,情感真挚;李清照的词则细腻哀婉,尤其擅长用词来表达复杂的情感。

唐诗和宋词不仅在中国受到极高的评价,也在世界范围内产生了深远的影响。它们的翻译作品广泛传播,让世界各地的读者都能感受到中国古典文学的魅力。这些诗词教会我们如何欣赏自然之美、理解人生的起落和体会情感的深浅。同时,它们也让我们更深入地了解中国的历史和文化。

阅读唐诗和宋词,我们不仅能学到优美的词句,还能理解它们背后的历史和文化内涵。通过这些诗歌,我们可以了解到古代人们的智慧和才华。

# Chinese Calligraphy
书法：超越文字魅力的艺术

## Listening & practice 听英文原声，完成练习

1. **What is Chinese calligraphy?**
   A. Writing on computers
   B. Special art of writing letters
   C. Painting pictures

2. **Which calligraphy style is very quick and free?**
   A. Regular script (楷书)
   B. Running script (行书)
   C. Cursive script (草书)

3. **Who is a famous calligrapher?**
   A. Wang Xizhi
   B. Li Bai
   C. Confucius

4. **What does calligraphy show?**
   A. How fast you can write
   B. Feelings and who you are
   C. Your favourite colour

5. **Why is learning calligraphy good?**
   A. It helps people appreciate beauty and learn patience
   B. It makes people strong
   C. It helps people run fast

## Reading 阅读下面的文章

Chinese **calligraphy** is a very special kind of art. It's not just about writing letters; it's a way to show feelings and smart ideas. Calligraphy has been around in China for **thousands of** years and is very important.

A long time ago, people started calligraphy with simple writing on bones and metal. As time went on, they created different styles like regular, running, **cursive**, and clerical **scripts**. Each style looks **unique** and beautiful.

Regular script is neat and easy to read. It's great for everyday writing. Running script is looser and faster, which makes it **flow** nicely. Cursive script is super quick and a bit hard to read because it's so free. Clerical script is in between, with its own special look.

Calligraphy is more than just good writing. It's full of deep meanings from the culture. In China, people use calligraphy to show their feelings and who they are. Every brush **stroke** tells something about the person who made it. That's why good calligraphy is not only beautiful to see but also feels special.

Famous calligraphers like Wang Xizhi and Yan Zhenqing used calligraphy to show their amazing art skills and deep **knowledge**. People still love and study their work today because it's so special.

Calligraphy is very respected in China and is seen as a fancy art. Learning calligraphy helps people appreciate beauty and learn **patience**. I hope everyone gets to try calligraphy to see how **wonderful** and wise it is.

## Vocabulary and phrases 词汇和短语

**calligraphy** [kə'lɪgrəfi] 名 书法
**cursive** ['kɜːsɪv] 形 草书的
**unique** [ju'niːk] 形 独特的
**stroke** [strəʊk] 名 一笔；一画
**patience** ['peɪʃns] 名 耐心；毅力

**thousands of** 短 数以千计的
**script** [skrɪpt] 名 字体
**flow** [fləʊ] 动 流动
**knowledge** ['nɒlɪdʒ] 名 知识；学问
**wonderful** ['wʌndəfl] 形 精彩的；极好的

## Practice  请选择合适的词填在下方的横线上

Calligraphy    scripts    patience    unique    flowing

1. There are many different _____ and styles of calligraphy.
2. In running script, the characters are written in a more _____ and connected manner compared to regular script.
3. Calligraphy can build _____ through practice.
4. _____ is the beautiful art of writing, where you can express your thoughts and feelings through your writing.
5. Each style of calligraphy has its _____ historical background and development history.

## Talking practice  情景对话模拟练习

玛丽和孙梅是一对好朋友,这一天她们讨论起中国的书法艺术,你也来跟着模拟这段对话吧。

Sun Mei, can you tell me about Chinese calligraphy?
孙梅,你能告诉我一些关于中国书法的事情吗?

Mary玛丽

Sun Mei孙梅

Sure! Chinese calligraphy is an old and special art form in China.
当然可以!中国书法是中国一种古老而特别的艺术形式。

How did calligraphy start?
书法是怎么开始的呢?

Mary玛丽

Sun Mei孙梅

It started with simple writing on bones and metal a long time ago.
很久以前,人们在骨头和金属上进行简单的书写,书法就这样开始了。

**What are the different styles of calligraphy?**
书法有哪些不同的风格?

Mary玛丽

Sun Mei孙梅

There are regular, running, cursive, and clerical scripts. Each one looks different.
有楷书、行书、草书和隶书。每一种看起来都不一样。

**Why is calligraphy important in China?**
书法在中国为什么重要?

Mary玛丽

Sun Mei孙梅

It's a way to show feelings and personality. Every brush stroke tells a story.
这是表达感情和个性的一种方式。每一笔画都讲述一个故事。

## Funny facts  关于书法的有趣事实和短语

**书法四体**：书法主要的四种基本字体是行书、隶书、楷书和草书。其中，楷书最为规范，草书最为自由奔放。

**文房四宝**：书法创作离不开"文房四宝"，即笔、墨、纸、砚。每一件工具都有其独特的制作工艺和使用方法，对书法作品的质量有着重要影响。

**书法大家**：历史上著名的书法家包括王羲之、颜真卿、柳公权、赵孟頫和苏轼等。他们的作品被视为书法艺术的巅峰，具有极高的艺术价值和收藏价值。

| | |
|---|---|
| **regular script** – 楷书 | **ink stone** – 砚台 |
| **running script** – 行书 | **ink stick** – 墨 |
| **cursive script** – 草书 | **ink wash** – 墨韵 |
| **seal script** – 篆书 | **calligraphy master** – 书法大家 |
| **seal** – 印章 | |

## Writing practice 写作小练习

**根据我们这一节所学到的内容，写出下面句子的英文。**

1. 中国书法有不同的风格。

2. 如果你喜欢汉字，可以学习书法。

3. 王羲之是中国历史上最有名的书法家之一。

## Reference translation 参考译文

中国传统书法是一种独特的艺术形式，它不仅仅是写字，更是一种情感和智慧的表达。书法在中国有着上千年的历史，其重要性不言而喻。

很久以前，人们开始在骨头和金属上书写简单的文字。随着时间的推移，书法发展出了不同的风格，包括楷书、行书、草书和隶书等。每一种书写风格都有其独特的特点和美学价值。

楷书整洁易读，非常适合日常书写。行书则更加随意快捷，书写流畅。草书速度极快，但因其自由奔放而略显难以辨认。隶书则介于行书和草书之间，具有独特的风格。

书法不仅仅是好的书写方式，它还蕴含了丰富的文化内涵。在中国，人们通过书法来表达自己的情感和个性。书写时的每一个笔触都反映了书法家的心境和性格。因此，好的书法作品不仅仅是视觉上的美，更是心灵上的触动。

中国的书法家们，如王羲之、颜真卿都是通过书法展示了他们的艺术才华和深厚的文化修养。他们的作品至今仍被人们所推崇和研究，因为它们具有独特的魅力。

书法在中国社会中有着极高的地位，被视为一种高雅的艺术。学习书法不仅可以提升个人的审美和文化素养，还能帮助培养耐心。我希望每个人都能尝试书法，感受它的美妙与智慧。

# Chinese Tea Culture
## 茶文化：悠闲的生活艺术

**Listening & practice** 听英文原声，完成练习

扫码听音频

1. **How long has Chinese tea culture been around?**
   A. Hundreds of years
   B. Thousands of years
   C. Tens of years

2. **What is Kung Fu tea?**
   A. A type of tea dance
   B. A special way of making tea in Guangdong and Fujian
   C. A tea fighting style

3. **Which tea gets better as it gets older?**
   A. Green tea
   B. Oolong tea
   C. Pu'er tea

4. **Where does Pu'er tea come from?**
   A. Guangdong
   B. Fujian
   C. Yunnan

5. **What does making and tasting tea help people do?**
   A. Run faster
   B. Get along better
   C. Sing better

## Reading   阅读下面的文章

Chinese tea culture is a big part of China's **traditions** and has been around for thousands of years. Long ago, people in China found tea and started drinking it for fun and during special ceremonies. Now, making and drinking tea is like an art.

Making tea is more than just **brewing** and drinking. It **involves** choosing the right tea leaves, knowing how to brew them well, and understanding how to enjoy the tea. In China, different places have their own ways of making tea. For example, in Guangdong and Fujian, people enjoy Kung Fu tea, which needs special tea sets and **careful** steps.

China has many kinds of tea, each with its own **taste**. Green tea is **common** and tastes fresh and clean, like Longjing from West Lake and Biluochun. Black tea is strong and popular in places like Fujian. Pu'er tea comes from Yunnan and gets better as it gets older.

There are also teas like Oolong, which **smells** great, and white tea, which is light and nice. Each type of tea has a rich history and culture.

In Chinese tea culture, brewing and tasting tea helps people get along better. It's not just about drinking tea, but also about enjoying time with **family** and friends.

There are also many stories and poems about tea in China. For example, Lu Yu from the Tang Dynasty wrote *The Classic of Tea*, the first detailed book about tea. It talks about different teas, how to make them, and poems about enjoying tea.

Now, Chinese tea culture is loved all over the world, and people from different **countries** enjoy this calm and peaceful way of living. Chinese tea is also known around the world as good for **health**, and people everywhere enjoy it.

## Vocabulary and phrases 词汇和短语

tradition [trəˈdɪʃn] 名 传统

involve [ɪnˈvɒlv] 动 包括

taste [teɪst] 名 味道 动 品尝

smell [smel] 动 闻;嗅

country [ˈkʌntri] 名 国家

brew [bruː] 动 泡（茶）

careful [ˈkeəfl] 形 小心的；谨慎的

common [ˈkɒmən] 形 平常的；普通的

family [ˈfæməli] 名 家庭

health [helθ] 名 健康

## Practice 请选择合适的词填在下方的横线上

tradition    tastes    common    health    smells

1. Chinese tea offers a wide range of _____ with its rich and malty flavour.

2. Drinking Chinese tea is not only a cultural tradition, but also a habit that is beneficial to _____.

3. Tea culture is an essential component (组成) of Chinese _____.

4. Tea is a _____ beverage (饮品) enjoyed worldwide.

5. Green tea _____ very fresh and fragrant.

## Talking practice 情景对话模拟练习

陈博邀请了外国朋友约翰一起喝茶,他们聊起了中国的茶文化,请你一起来模拟这段对话吧。

John 约翰

**This tea is really good, Chen Bo! What kind of tea is it?**
陈博,这茶真好喝!这是什么茶?

Chen Bo 陈博

**It's Longjing tea from West Lake. It's a type of green tea.**
这是西湖的龙井茶,是一种绿茶。

John 约翰

**Can you tell me more about Chinese tea culture?**
你能给我讲讲中国茶文化吗?

Chen Bo 陈博

**Sure! Tea culture in China is very old and important. It's like an art.**
当然可以!中国的茶文化非常古老和重要。它就像一种艺术。

John 约翰

**What are some other types of Chinese tea?**
还有哪些种类的中国茶?

Chen Bo 陈博

**There are many, like black tea, Oolong tea, white tea, and Pu'er tea.**
有很多,比如红茶、乌龙茶、白茶和普洱茶。

John 约翰

**How do people in China usually make tea?**
中国人通常怎么泡茶?

In different places, they have special ways. For example, in Guangdong, they use Kung Fu tea sets.
在不同的地方，他们有特别的方法。比如在广东，他们用功夫茶具。

Chen Bo 陈博

That's interesting! I want to learn more about tea.
那真有趣！我想了解更多关于茶的知识。

John 约翰

## Funny facts  关于茶文化的有趣事实和短语

**六大类**：中国茶主要分为六大类：绿茶、红茶、白茶、黄茶、青茶（乌龙茶）和黑茶，每一种茶都有其独特的制作工艺和风味。

**茶圣陆羽**：唐代的陆羽被誉为"茶圣"，他所著的《茶经》是世界上第一部关于茶的专著，详细介绍了茶的种植、采摘、制作和饮用方法。

**功夫茶**：起源于福建和广东地区的功夫茶是一种讲究技艺和仪式感的泡茶方式，通常用于招待贵客。功夫茶注重泡茶的每一个细节，包括茶叶的选择、水温的控制和茶具的使用。

| | |
|---|---|
| **tea ceremony** – 茶道 | **yellow tea** – 黄茶 |
| **green tea** – 绿茶 | **tea master** – 茶艺师 |
| **black tea** – 红茶 | **tea set** – 茶具 |
| **Oolong tea** – 乌龙茶 | **Kung Fu tea** – 功夫茶 |
| **white tea** – 白茶 | **tea house** – 茶馆 |

## Writing practice  写作小练习

根据我们这一节所学到的内容，写出下面句子的英文。

1. 在中国，品茶不仅是一种生活方式，更是一种艺术。

   _____

2. 中国茶主要分为六大类：绿茶、红茶、白茶、黄茶、乌龙茶和黑茶。

   _____

3. 在广东，人们更喜欢喝功夫茶。

## Reference translation 参考译文

中国茶艺文化是中国传统文化的重要组成部分，拥有几千年的历史。很早以前，中国人发现了茶叶，并开始在各种场合和特殊仪式中饮用。如今，泡茶和品茶已成为一种艺术。

茶艺不仅仅是泡茶和喝茶那么简单，它还包括了选择茶叶、泡茶的技巧以及品茶的方式。在中国，不同的地区有着各自独特的泡茶方式。比如在广东和福建，人们喜欢功夫茶，这需要特殊的茶具和细致的步骤。

中国的茶叶种类也很多，每种茶叶都有其独特的风味。绿茶是较为常见的一种，口感清新，如西湖龙井和碧螺春。红茶口味浓郁，在福建非常流行。普洱茶来自云南，而且越陈越香。

还有像乌龙茶这样香气扑鼻的茶叶，以及口感清淡的白茶。每种茶叶都蕴含着丰富的历史和文化。

在中国茶文化中，泡茶和品茶有助于人们更好地相处。在品茶时，人们不仅享受茶的味道，更享受与家人和朋友聚会的欢乐时光。

中国茶文化中还包括了很多关于茶的故事和诗词。例如，唐代的陆羽写了《茶经》，这是世界上第一本全面系统地介绍茶的书籍。书中不仅介绍了茶的种类和制作方法，还有很多关于如何品茶和享受茶的美妙诗句。

今天，中国的茶文化受到全世界人民的喜爱，许多国家的人们也开始喜欢和欣赏这种悠闲和宁静的生活方式。在国际上，中国茶也被视为健康和养生的代表，深受各地人们的喜爱。

# Chinese Silk
## 丝绸：柔软高贵的典范

**Listening & practice** 听英文原声，完成练习

▶扫码听音频◀

1. Who discovered silk in China?

    A. An emperor

    B. An empress named Leizu

    C. A farmer

2. What is the Silk Road?

    A. A trade route linking the East and West

    B. A modern highway

    C. A river in China

3. What is Chinese silk known for?

    A. Being rough and dull

    B. Being made of cotton

    C. Being soft, smooth, and colourful

4. What did people trade on the Silk Road?

    A. Only silk

    B. Silk, spices, tea, and gold and silver

    C. Only animals

5. Where did the Silk Road start?

    A. Beijing

    B. Chang'an

    C. Shanghai

## Reading 阅读下面的文章

Chinese silk is a very beautiful and special **fabric** that has been around for thousands of years. It's soft, smooth, and very colourful, which is why ancient Chinese emperors and **nobles** loved it.

China was the first place to make silk. A long time ago, an empress named Leizu discovered silk when she saw a **silkworm** making it. She decided to try **weaving** the silk threads into cloth, and that's how silk started. Later on, Chinese people learned how to raise silkworms and make silk even better.

Silk was not just popular in China, but it also **traveled** far along a trade route called the Silk Road. The Silk Road was **a bunch of** old paths that linked the East and West, starting from a place called Chang'an in China, all the way to Rome by the sea.

The Silk Road helped people from different places share things with each other. Chinese silk, along with **spices**, tea, gold and silver, went to places like Europe and the Middle East. Meanwhile, horses, rare animals, and **jewelry** from the West came into China.

Making Chinese silk involves a lot of careful steps, from taking care of silkworms to spinning the silk and weaving it into fabric. This careful work makes Chinese silk really high **quality** and famous around the world.

Today, Chinese silk is still a very important part of Chinese culture. It's not just famous because it's old, but also because it shows the **cleverness** and **artistic** skills of Chinese people. The softness and **shine** of silk make it a fabric that people all over the world love.

## Vocabulary and phrases 词汇和短语

fabric ['fæbrɪk] 名 织物；织品

silkworm ['sɪlkwɜːm] 名 蚕

travel ['trævl] 动 传播；旅游

spice [spaɪs] 名 香料

quality ['kwɒləti] 名 质量

artistic [ɑːˈtɪstɪk] 形 艺术的

noble ['nəʊbl] 名 贵族

weave [wiːv] 动 编织；织

a bunch of 短 很多

jewelry ['dʒuːəlrɪ] 名 珠宝

cleverness ['klevənəs] 名 聪明；机灵

shine [ʃaɪn] 名 光泽

## Practice 请选择合适的词填在下方的横线上

fabric   nobles   silkworms   shine   artistic

1. The _____ of silk is a result of the way light interacts with the fibres.

2. Silk is a natural _____ that has been treasured for thousands of years.

3. Silk possesses extremely high _____ value.

4. Silk is produced by _____, small creatures that feed on mulberry leaves.

5. In ancient times, silk was often worn by _____ and members of the royal family.

丝绸：柔软高贵的典范

## Talking practice 情景对话模拟练习

凯特和苏敏正在谈论关于丝绸之路的有趣话题，你能跟着一起练习对话吗？

Kate凯特

Su Min, I heard about the Silk Road. Can you tell me more about it?
苏敏，我听说过丝绸之路。你能告诉我更多吗？

Su Min苏敏

Sure! The Silk Road was a bunch of old paths that connected China to Europe and the Middle East.
当然可以！丝绸之路是一条连接中国与欧洲和中东的古老通道。

Kate凯特

Why is it called the Silk Road?
为什么叫丝绸之路呢？

Su Min苏敏

It's called the Silk Road because Chinese silk was a big part of the trade along this route.
叫丝绸之路是因为中国丝绸是这条路上贸易的重要部分。

Kate凯特

What else was traded on the Silk Road?
丝绸之路上还有什么东西被交易呢？

Su Min苏敏

Besides silk, there were spices, tea, gold and silver going to the West. From the West, we got horses, rare animals, and jewelry.
除了丝绸，还有香料、茶叶、金银运往西方。从西方，我们得到了马、珍稀动物和珠宝。

Kate凯特

That's so interesting! How did Chinese people make silk?
那真有趣！中国人是怎么制作丝绸的？

Su Min 苏敏

They raised silkworms, spun the silk threads, and then wove them into fabric. It takes a lot of careful work.
他们养蚕、纺丝，然后把丝线织成布料。这需要很多精心的工作。

Wow, no wonder Chinese silk is so famous and beautiful!
哇，难怪中国丝绸如此有名又美丽！

Kate 凯特

### Funny facts 关于丝绸的有趣事实和短语

养蚕缫丝：养蚕是一个复杂的过程，需要细心照料蚕的生长并从蚕茧中提取丝线。一个蚕茧可以拉出平均约1000米长的蚕丝。

地位的象征：丝绸在中国文化中象征着富贵和高雅。古代皇室和贵族常穿着丝绸服装，以显示他们的身份和地位。

马可·波罗：意大利旅行家马可·波罗在13世纪通过丝绸之路到达中国，他的旅行见闻后来写成《马可·波罗游记》，在欧洲引起了对东方的极大兴趣。

| | |
|---|---|
| **mulberry leaves** – 桑叶 | **Yumen Pass** – 玉门关 |
| **silk embroidery** – 丝绸刺绣 | **Marco Polo** – 马可·波罗 |
| **brocade** – 锦缎 | **caravan** – 商队 |

### Writing practice 写作小练习

根据我们这一节所学到的内容，写出下面句子的英文。

1. 丝绸摸起来非常柔软，所以常常用来制作服装。

   _____

2. 丝绸不仅美丽，还含有重要的文化意义。

   _____

3. 丝绸之路是一条连接中国和西方的重要商道。

   _____

# Reference translation 参考译文

中国丝绸是一种非常美丽而特别的织物,已有数千年的历史。丝绸柔软、光滑且色彩丰富,因此被古代中国的皇帝和贵族们所喜爱。

中国是最早制作丝绸的国家。很久以前,传说一位名叫嫘祖的皇后,在看到蚕吐丝时发现了丝绸。她决定尝试将蚕丝编织成布,这就是丝绸的起源。后来,中国人学会了如何饲养蚕并制作出更好的丝绸。

丝绸不仅在中国非常受欢迎,还通过一条名为"丝绸之路"的贸易路线传播到了世界各地。丝绸之路是一系列古老的商路,连接了东方和西方,从中国的长安出发,一直延伸到地中海的罗马。

丝绸之路帮助了来自不同地方的人们相互分享。中国的丝绸与香料、茶叶、金银器等商品一起,被运送到了欧洲、中东等地。与此同时,西方的马匹、稀有的动物和珠宝被运进中国。

制作中国丝绸需要经过许多精心的步骤,从照顾蚕宝宝到纺丝和织成织物。这项细致的工作使中国丝绸具有高品质,并在世界各地享有盛誉。

如今,中国丝绸仍然是中国文化中非常重要的一部分。不仅因为它的历史悠久,也因为它体现了中国人民的智慧和艺术才能。丝绸的柔软和光泽使其成为世界各地人们喜爱的织物。

# Chinese Paper-cut
## 剪纸艺术：民间艺术的代表

**Listening & practice** 听英文原声，完成练习

扫码听音频

1. How long has Chinese paper-cut been around?
    A. Over 1,400 years
    B. Over 1,000 years
    C. Over 500 years

2. What do people use to make paper-cuts?
    A. Pens and pencils
    B. Scissors or knives
    C. Brushes and ink

3. What do dragons and phoenixes in paper-cuts stand for?
    A. Luck and health
    B. Happiness and joy
    C. Power and greatness

4. When is paper-cut often used for decorations?
    A. During Chinese New Year and other festivals
    B. During summer holidays
    C. During sports events

5. What did UNESCO call Chinese paper-cut?
    A. A famous painting
    B. An Intangible Cultural Heritage of Humanity
    C. A modern art

## Reading 阅读下面的文章

Chinese paper-cut is a fun art that's been around for over 1,400 years. It uses scissors or knives to make different shapes with paper. These shapes often mean things like luck, health, or celebrating good times in life.

Paper-cut started in the sixth century during the Northern and Southern Dynasties. People used paper-cuts to decorate doors and windows to keep away bad spirits and bring peace. By the Tang and Song Dynasties, paper-cut was really popular and used to decorate more things like statues, gifts, and lanterns.

What's cool about paper-cut is that it's simple but can show a lot. A plain piece of red or coloured paper can be turned into exciting pictures of flowers, animals, or people by skilled artists. These paper-cuts are often put up during Chinese New Year and other festivals to make things more festive and fun.

Paper-cut is more than just art. It has deep meanings. For example, dragons and phoenixes in paper-cuts stand for power and greatness, while lotus flowers and fish mean purity and plenty. Paper-cut shows how much Chinese people love nature and life and their hopes for a great future.

Because paper-cut is so special and means so much, UNESCO calls it an Intangible Cultural Heritage of Humanity. Today, paper-cut is still part of many Chinese celebrations and more and more people around the world

love it. I hope everyone can see the beauty and depth of Chinese culture through paper-cut art.

## Vocabulary and phrases 词汇和短语

scissors [ˈsɪzəz] 名 剪刀

decorate [ˈdekəreɪt] 动 装饰

plain [pleɪn] 形 简单的；平常的

festive [ˈfestɪv] 形 节日的；喜庆的

greatness [ˈgreɪtnəs] 名 伟大

celebration [ˌselɪˈbreɪʃn] 名 典礼；庆祝

shape [ʃeɪp] 名 形状

lantern [ˈlæntən] 名 灯笼

put up 短 张贴

phoenix [ˈfiːnɪks] 名 凤凰

humanity [hjuːˈmænəti] 名 人类

## Practice 请选择合适的词填在下方的横线上

scissors   shapes   decorate   festive   put up

1. The _____ can be anything from flowers and animals to scenes of daily life.

2. The art of paper-cut began as a way to _____ windows.

3. Many people enjoy to _____ paper-cuts _____ on walls, windows, doors, or any flat surface.

4. Paper-cuts are widely used to create a _____ atmosphere.

5. Artists use _____ or special knives to cut intricate designs into paper.

## Talking practice 情景对话模拟练习

温迪和好朋友安妮聊起了她在中国的见闻，你也来跟着一起练习这段对话吧。

**Wendy, did you learn anything interesting in China?**
温迪，你在中国学到了什么有趣的东西吗？

Annie安妮

Wendy温迪

**Yes, I learned about Chinese paper-cut. It's a fun and old art form.**
是的，我学到了关于中国剪纸的知识。这是一种有趣而古老的艺术形式。

**What is paper-cut?**
什么是剪纸？

Annie安妮

Wendy温迪

**It's when you use scissors or knives to make different shapes with paper. These shapes often mean things like luck and health.**
就是用剪刀或刀在纸上剪出不同的形状。这些形状通常意味着好运和健康。

**When did Chinese people start doing paper-cut?**
中国人什么时候开始剪纸的？

Annie安妮

Wendy温迪

**It started over 1,400 years ago during the Northern and Southern Dynasties.**
它始于1,400多年前的南北朝时期。

**What do people use paper-cuts for?**
人们用剪纸做什么呢？

Annie安妮

Wendy温迪

They use them to decorate doors and windows, especially during festivals like Chinese New Year.
他们用剪纸装饰门窗,尤其是在春节等节日期间。

That's cool! What do the shapes mean?
那真酷!这些形状有什么含义?

Annie安妮

Wendy温迪

Shapes like dragons and phoenixes stand for power and greatness, while lotus flowers and fish mean purity and rich.
像龙和凤凰这样的形状象征着力量和伟大,而莲花和鱼象征着纯洁和富足。

## Funny facts 关于剪纸艺术的有趣事实和短语

技法多样:剪纸技法多样,包括单色剪纸、多色剪纸、折叠剪纸、镂空剪纸等。每种技法都能创造出独特的视觉效果。

寓意吉祥:剪纸作品常常蕴含吉祥寓意,如"喜鹊登梅"象征喜事临门,"莲年有鱼"寓意连年有余,"双喜临门"代表婚庆等。

| | |
|---|---|
| **window flower** – 窗花 | **dragon and phoenix** – 龙凤 |
| **symmetrical pattern** – 对称图案 | **folk art** – 民间艺术 |
| **double happiness** – 双喜 | **longevity** – 长寿 |

## Writing practice 写作小练习

根据我们这一节所学到的内容,写出下面句子的英文。

1. 剪纸是一种有趣且古老的艺术。

2. 剪纸就是用剪刀或刀在纸上剪出不同的形状。

3. 在中国传统文化中，龙代表着力量，鱼代表着富有。

## Reference translation 参考译文

中国传统剪纸艺术是一种已经流传了1,400多年的有趣的民间艺术。剪纸是用剪刀或刻刀在纸上剪刻出各种图案。这些图案通常意味着好运、健康或庆祝生活中的美好时光。

剪纸的历史可以追溯到公元六世纪的南北朝时期。当时人们开始用剪纸来装饰门窗，希望通过这种方式来祛邪保平安。到了唐宋时期，剪纸艺术已经非常流行，并且开始用作更多的装饰用途，如装饰神像、礼品和灯笼。

剪纸艺术的特色在于它简单但表达力强。一张普通的红色或彩色纸张，经过艺术家巧妙的设计与剪切，便可以变成生动的花朵、动物、人物图案。这些剪纸作品通常在中国新年和其他传统节日中被张贴起来，用来增添节日的气氛和欢乐。

剪纸不仅仅是一种艺术，它还承载着深远的意义。例如，剪纸中常见的龙和凤的图案象征着权力和贵气，而剪出的莲花和鱼则分别代表了纯洁和富裕。剪纸艺术传递了中国人对自然和生活的热爱及其对美好未来的祝愿。

由于剪纸如此特别且意义重大，联合国教科文组织将其列为人类非物质文化遗产。如今，剪纸仍然是许多中国庆祝活动的一部分，并且越来越多的人喜欢它。希望大家能通过剪纸艺术，感受到中国文化的魅力和深度。

# Part 3
# 中国的传统节日和节气

# The Spring Festival
春节：辞旧迎新又一年

## Listening & practice  听英文原声，完成练习

▶扫码听音频◀

1. When does the Spring Festival usually start?
   A. In December
   B. In January or February
   C. In March

2. What was the monster "Nian" afraid of?
   A. Red colour and loud sounds
   B. Water and wind
   C. Darkness and silence

3. What do families do to prepare for the Spring Festival?
   A. Go on vacation
   B. Clean their house and hang red lanterns
   C. Paint their house

4. What do people eat on Chinese New Year's Eve?
   A. Pizza and burgers
   B. Fish, dumplings, and rice cakes
   C. Bread and soup

5. What do kids get from older family members during the Spring Festival?
   A. Toys
   B. Books
   C. Red envelopes with money

## Reading 阅读下面的文章

The Spring Festival, also called Chinese New Year, is one of China's biggest and most important festivals. It starts on the first day of the lunar calendar, usually in January or February. The Spring Festival is more than just a holiday; it's a time for fresh starts and family gatherings.

Long ago, the Spring Festival started because of an old story about a monster named "Nian" who was scared of the colour red and loud sounds. People used firecrackers and red things to scare "Nian" away. That's why using firecrackers and hanging red couplets became a tradition.

During the Spring Festival, every family cleans their house really well to sweep away the old and welcome the new. After cleaning, they hang red lanterns and red couplets that have good wishes written on them. Everyone wears new clothes, especially red ones, because red is a lucky colour in Chinese culture.

On Chinese New Year's Eve, which is the night before the Chinese New Year, families have a big dinner together. They eat fish, dumplings, and rice cakes. Fish means having more than enough every year. Dumplings look like ancient treasures and symbolize wealth. Rice cakes mean getting higher or doing better each year.

During the Spring Festival, kids love getting red envelopes with money from older family members. This is a way to share good luck and blessings. People also set off fireworks to celebrate the new year and to chase away bad things.

The Spring Festival isn't just for fun; it's also about families coming together and sharing love and kindness. During this festival, no matter where people are, they try to go home and be with their families.

This shows how much family means in Chinese culture and how everyone **looks forward to** the new year with hope.

## Vocabulary and phrases 词汇和短语

calendar [ˈkælɪndə(r)] 名 日历

firecracker [ˈfaɪəkrækə(r)] 名 爆竹；鞭炮

dumpling [ˈdʌmplɪŋ] 名 饺子

envelope [ˈenvələʊp] 名 信封

look forward to 短 期待

monster [ˈmɒnstə(r)] 名 怪物

sweep away 短 扫除；清除掉

symbolize [ˈsɪmbəlaɪz] 动 象征

blessing [ˈblesɪŋ] 名 祝福

## Practice 请选择合适的词填在下方的横线上

festival    calendar    sweep away    envelopes    dumplings

1. Before the Spring Festival, people usually do a thorough cleaning of their homes to _____ bad luck from the previous year.

2. On the first day of the new year, children receive red _____ with money from elders.

3. The festival typically starts on the first day of the lunar _____.

4. We always make _____ for the Spring Festival!

5. The Spring Festival is the most important traditional _____ in the country.

## Talking practice 情景对话模拟练习

乔治第一次来到中国，对春节很感兴趣，王迪告诉了他关于春节的有趣知识。

Wang Di, can you tell me about the Spring Festival?
王迪，你能告诉我一些关于春节的事情吗？

George乔治

Wang Di王迪

Sure! The Spring Festival, also called Chinese New Year, is one of the most important festivals in China.
当然可以！春节，也叫中国新年，是中国最重要的节日之一。

When does it start?
它什么时候开始？

George乔治

Wang Di王迪

It starts on the first day of the lunar calendar, usually in January or February.
它在农历的第一天开始，通常在1月或2月。

What do people do to celebrate?
人们怎么庆祝呢？

George乔治

Wang Di王迪

We clean our houses, hang red lanterns and couplets, and wear new clothes. Red is a lucky colour.
我们打扫房子、挂红灯笼和贴对联、穿新衣服。红色是幸运色。

What do you eat during the festival?
你们在节日期间吃什么？

George乔治

Wang Di 王迪

We eat fish, dumplings, and rice cakes. Fish means having more than enough, dumplings mean wealth, and rice cakes mean getting better each year.
我们吃鱼、饺子和年糕。鱼代表年年有余，饺子象征财富，年糕意味着年年高升。

What do kids like the most about the Spring Festival?
孩子们最喜欢春节的什么？

George 乔治

Wang Di 王迪

Kids love getting red envelopes with money from older family members. It's a way to share good luck and blessings.
孩子们喜欢从长辈那里得到装有钱的红包。这是一种分享好运和祝福的方式。

## Funny facts  关于春节的有趣事实和短语

春联和福字：春节期间，家家户户会在门口贴上春联和倒贴福字，寓意新年的吉祥和福气到来。

守岁：除夕夜有守岁的传统，家人们一起熬夜迎接新年的到来，寓意着辞旧迎新。

逛庙会：春节期间，各地会举办庙会，展示传统的民间艺术和手工艺品，同时还有各种美食摊位和娱乐活动，吸引大量游客前来参与。

**lunar calendar** – 农历
**Chinese New Year's Eve** – 除夕夜
**reunion dinner** – 年夜饭
**red envelope** – 红包
**lucky money** – 压岁钱

**Spring Festival couplets** – 春联
**the Spring Festival Gala** – 春节联欢晚会
**temple fair** – 庙会

## Writing practice 写作小练习

**根据我们这一节所学到的内容，写出下面句子的英文。**

1. 春节是新的一年的开始，也是中国最重要的传统节日。

2. 春节的时候，人们会穿上新衣服，走亲访友。

3. 孩子们会从家长那里得到压岁钱。

## Reference translation 参考译文

　　春节，又称为中国新年，是中国最大、最重要的节日之一。它始于农历正月初一，通常在1月或2月。春节不仅仅是一个节日，更是一个新的开始和家庭团聚的时刻。

　　很久以前，春节的起源于一个关于名为"年"的怪兽的古老故事。这个怪兽害怕红色和响亮的声音，因此人们用鞭炮和红色的东西来吓跑"年"。这就是为什么放鞭炮和贴红对联成为了一种传统。

　　春节期间，每个家庭都会彻底打扫房屋，以扫除旧岁、迎接新春。打扫干净后，他们会挂红灯笼贴红对联，上面写满了美好的祝福语。家里的每个人都会穿上新衣服，特别是红色的衣服，因为红色在中国文化中代表着幸运和喜庆。

　　除夕之夜，即新年前夜，家人们会聚在一起享用丰盛的晚餐。他们吃鱼、饺子和年糕。鱼代表"年年有余"，饺子形状像古代的金元宝，象征财富，年糕则寓意"年年高升"或"越来越好"。

　　春节期间，孩子们喜欢从长辈那里收到装有钱的红包。这是一种分享好运和祝福的方式。人们还会燃放烟花爆竹来庆祝新年，并驱走不好的东西。

　　春节不仅仅是庆祝，它还是家人团聚、表达亲情和友好的时刻。在这个节日里，无论人们身在何处，都会设法回家与家人共度。这样的传统展现了中国文化中对家庭的重视和对新一年的希望与期待。

# The Lantern Festival
## 元宵节：团团圆圆的节日

**Listening & practice** 听英文原声，完成练习

扫码听音频

1. **When is the Lantern Festival celebrated?**
   A. On the first day of the lunar month
   B. On the fifteenth day of the first month in the Chinese lunar calendar
   C. On the tenth day of the lunar month

2. **What do people enjoy during the Lantern Festival?**
   A. Watching lanterns and solving riddles
   B. Eating zongzi
   C. Swimming

3. **What special food do people eat during the Lantern Festival?**
   A. Dumplings
   B. Mooncakes
   C. Yuanxiao or tangyuan

4. **Why do dragon and lion dance during the Lantern Festival?**
   A. Show strength
   B. Scare away bad luck and bring good luck
   C. Tell stories

5. **What do round yuanxiao or tangyuan mean?**
   A. Wealth and power
   B. Strength and health
   C. Togetherness and happiness

## Reading 阅读下面的文章

The Lantern Festival, is a special Chinese festival celebrated on the fifteenth day of the first month in the Chinese lunar calendar every year. It marks the end of the Spring Festival celebrations. This festival started a long time ago during the Han Dynasty when people began to light lanterns to **honour** Buddha.

During the Lantern Festival, people enjoy watching beautiful lanterns, **solving** fun riddles that are written on the lanterns, and eating a special food called yuanxiao or tangyuan. Lanterns are a big part of this festival. They are in many shapes and colours and are **hung** in streets, alleys, and homes. There are also big fairs where people go to see lots of lanterns and try to guess the answers to **riddles**.

Eating yuanxiao or tangyuan is another important custom of this festival. These are **sticky** rice balls with sweet fillings like bean paste or sesame. They are round, which means **togetherness** and **happiness**, hoping that families will stay close and happy.

There are also exciting dragon and lion dances during the Lantern Festival. These dances are **performed** to scare away bad luck and bring good luck and peace for the new year. Kids **really** love watching these big and colourful dances.

When the Lantern Festival comes, Chinese people everywhere celebrate with these **activities**, enjoying the beauty and warmth of their traditions.

The Lantern Festival is a big part of Chinese culture. It shows how much Chinese people enjoy life and have good hopes for the future. With all these traditions, they share their dreams for a great life and show love for their families.

## Vocabulary and phrases 词汇和短语

honour [ˈɒnə(r)] 动 尊敬；敬意

hang [hæŋ] 动 悬挂

sticky [ˈstɪki] 形 黏的

happiness [ˈhæpinəs] 名 幸福

really [ˈriːəli] 副 真正地

solve [sɒlv] 动 解答；解开

riddle [ˈrɪdl] 名 谜；谜语

togetherness [təˈɡeðənəs] 名 相聚；团聚

perform [pəˈfɔːm] 动 表演

activity [ækˈtɪvɪti] 名 活动

## Practice 请选择合适的词填在下方的横线上

riddles    sticky    togetherness    activities    hang

1. During the Lantern Festival, families _____ colourful lanterns, and the streets are filled with joy and festive atmosphere.

2. Eating yuanxiao symbolizes _____ and harmony.

3. There is a tradition of guessing lantern _____ during the Lantern Festival.

4. One of the most interesting _____ during the Lantern Festival is to admire the beautiful lanterns.

5. Yuanxiao is a sweet dessert made of _____ rice flour, filled with sesame, red bean paste, and more.

## Talking practice 情景对话模拟练习

辛迪对中国传统的元宵节非常感兴趣,她正好遇到了同学张华,他们展开了这段对话。

**Zhang Hua, I heard about the Lantern Festival. Can you tell me more about it?**
张华,我听说过元宵节。你能告诉我更多吗?

Cindy 辛迪

Zhang Hua 张华
**Sure! The Lantern Festival is celebrated on the fifteenth day of the first month in the Chinese lunar calendar. It marks the end of the Spring Festival.**
当然可以!元宵节在农历正月十五庆祝,是春节的结束。

**What do people do to celebrate the Lantern Festival?**
人们如何庆祝元宵节呢?

Cindy 辛迪

Zhang Hua 张华
**We look at beautiful lanterns, guess riddles on them, and eat special food called yuanxiao or tangyuan.**
我们欣赏美丽的灯笼,猜灯谜,还吃一种特别的食物,叫作元宵或汤圆。

**What are yuanxiao or tangyuan?**
元宵或汤圆是什么?

Cindy 辛迪

Zhang Hua 张华
**They are sticky rice balls with sweet fillings. They represent togetherness and happiness.**
它们是有甜馅的糯米球,象征着团圆和幸福。

**Are there any special performances during the festival?**
节日期间有特别的表演吗?

Cindy 辛迪

Zhang Hua 张华
**Yes, we have dragon and lion dances to scare away bad luck and bring good luck for the new year.**
有的,我们有舞龙舞狮表演,来驱赶厄运并为新年带来好运。

## Funny facts  关于元宵节的有趣事实和短语

闹元宵：每到农历正月十五，人们会击鼓鸣锣，通宵张灯，还会舞龙舞狮，热闹非凡，所以也称为"闹元宵"。

赏花灯：元宵节的重要活动之一是赏花灯。各地会制作各式各样的彩灯，悬挂在街道、庭院和公园，灯笼形状丰富多彩，有龙灯、鱼灯、人物灯等。

猜灯谜：猜灯谜是元宵节的传统活动之一。灯谜通常写在纸条上，贴在花灯上供人猜测，既增加了节日的趣味性，又考验了人们的智慧。

lantern display – 灯展
riddles on lanterns – 灯谜
dragon dance – 舞龙

lion dance – 舞狮
sky lanterns – 天灯
lantern parade – 花灯游行

## Writing practice  写作小练习

根据我们这一节所学到的内容，写出下面句子的英文。

1. 人们会在街上漫步，欣赏这些美丽的花灯。

2. 猜灯谜是元宵节的一个传统习俗。

3. 元宵是元宵节的传统美食。

## Reference translation 参考译文

元宵节是中国的传统节日之一,每年农历正月十五庆祝,标志着春节活动的结束。这个节日的历史非常悠久,起源于汉代,当时人们开始点灯祭祀佛祖。

在元宵节期间,人们喜欢观赏美丽的灯笼,解答灯笼上写的有趣灯谜,并吃一种叫作元宵或汤圆的特殊食物。灯笼是这个节日的重要组成部分,它们形状各异、色彩斑斓,被悬挂在街道、小巷和家中。此外,还有大型灯会,人们可以前往观赏众多灯笼并尝试猜解灯谜的答案。

吃元宵或汤圆是元宵节的重要传统。元宵和汤圆是用糯米制成的,内有甜馅(如豆沙或芝麻)。它们的圆形象征团圆和完整,寓意全家人团团圆圆,和和美美。

元宵节期间还有激动人心的舞龙舞狮表演。这些传统活动寓意祛邪避祸,带来新一年的好运和平安。孩子们特别喜欢观看这些色彩鲜艳、气势磅礴的舞龙舞狮。

每当元宵节来临,无论身在何处,中国人都会用这些方式来庆祝,感受传统文化的魅力和温暖。

元宵节不仅是中国文化的重要组成部分,也是展现中国人民热爱生活和追求美好愿景的节日。通过这些传统习俗,人们表达了对未来美好生活的期待和对家人的爱。

# The Tomb-sweeping Day
清明节：祭祖踏青的好时节

**Listening & practice** 听英文原声，完成练习

▶扫码听音频◀

1. When does the Tomb-sweeping Day happen?
   A. In early March
   B. In early April
   C. In early May

2. What do families do to show love and respect for their ancestors (祖先)?
   A. Clean graves and put flowers, food, and paper money on them
   B. Have a big party
   C. Paint pictures

3. What is one outdoor activity people do during the Tomb-sweeping Day?
   A. Swimming
   B. Going on trips to see nature
   C. Skiing

4. What do some kites have that make a sound?
   A. Little bells
   B. Small drums
   C. Tiny whistles

5. Why do people fly kites during the Tomb-sweeping Day?
   A. Making new friends
   B. Winning a race
   C. Sending away bad luck and bringing good health

## Reading 阅读下面的文章

The Tomb-sweeping Day happens in early April and is a special day in China. It's a time when families remember their ancestors by visiting and cleaning their graves.

The traditional Chinese term for the Tomb-sweeping Day is Pure Brightness (Qingming). It signals when spring is in full swing and all of nature is waking up. During this time, the weather warms up and plants begin to grow. It's the perfect time to go outside and think about ancestors.

On this day, families clean up around graves, and put flowers, food, and paper money on them to show love and respect for those who came before them. This tradition is very old and shows how much families care about their history and life.

Besides cleaning graves, people also enjoy going out into nature. Spring is a time when everything in nature starts to grow again. Families go on trips to see the beautiful outdoors, which is a way to celebrate life and look forward to the year to come.

Pure Brightness is also a time for flying kites. In some places, especially in the north, families fly kites together. Some kites have little bells that ring in the air, which is fun to hear. People think that flying kites can help send away bad luck and bring good health and safety.

The Tomb-sweeping Day is not only about remembering the past. It also helps people enjoy today and hope for the future. Through special activities on this day, everyone can feel close to their family and happy about the start of spring.

## Vocabulary and phrases 词汇和短语

remember [rɪˈmembə(r)] 动 铭记；回忆

grave [greɪv] 名 坟墓

spring [sprɪŋ] 名 春天

respect [rɪˈspekt] 名 尊重；敬重

kite [kaɪt] 名 风筝

ancestor [ˈænsestə(r)] 名 祖宗；祖先

signal [ˈsɪgnəl] 动 预示

wake up 短 醒来；苏醒

outdoors [ˌaʊtˈdɔːz] 名 户外

future [ˈfjuːtʃə(r)] 名 未来

## Practice 请选择合适的词填在下方的横线上

ancestors    graves    remember    respect    wakes up

1. On the Tomb-sweeping Day, we _____ our ancestors.

2. We express our _____ and gratitude (感激) to our ancestors through this way.

3. On the Tomb-sweeping Day, families gather together to honour and remember their _____.

4. They clear away any weeds or debris to ensure that the _____ are tidy and respectful.

5. The Tomb-sweeping Day falls in the spring season, when everything _____ and the earth gradually revives.

## Talking practice 情景对话模拟练习

菲奥娜对清明节不是很了解，于是她向自己的朋友陈琳请教，请你一起来跟着练习这段对话吧。

Chen Lin, what is the Tomb-sweeping Day?
陈琳，什么是清明节？

Fiona菲奥娜

Chen Lin陈琳

The Tomb-sweeping Day happens in early April. It's a time to remember our ancestors.
清明节在4月初，是我们纪念祖先的时间。

What do you do on this day?
这一天你们做什么呢？

Fiona菲奥娜

Chen Lin陈琳

We visit and clean the graves of our ancestors. We also put flowers and food on the graves.
我们去扫墓，清理祖先的坟墓。我们还会在坟上放花和食物。

What else do you do during this day?
在清明节期间，你们还做些什么？

Fiona菲奥娜

Chen Lin陈琳

We enjoy going out into nature and sometimes fly kites. It's a way to celebrate spring.
我们喜欢出去亲近大自然，有时会放风筝。这是庆祝春天的一种方式。

Why do people fly kites during the Tomb-sweeping Day?
为什么人们在清明节放风筝？

Fiona菲奥娜

Chen Lin陈琳

Flying kites can help send away bad luck and bring good health and safety.
放风筝可以祛赶厄运，带来健康和平安。

## Funny facts  关于清明节的有趣事实和短语

**传统食品**：清明节的传统食品——青团，是一种用艾草汁和糯米粉制成的绿色糕点，象征春天的气息。

**寒食节**：清明节前一天是"寒食节"，传说源于春秋时期晋文公为纪念介子推而设立的禁火节日，要求家家户户不生火做饭，只吃冷食。

**清明上河图**：北宋画家张择端的《清明上河图》描绘了北宋汴京清明时节的繁荣景象，是中国古代绘画的杰作之一。

**grave cleaning** – 扫墓  
**spring outing** – 踏青  
**ancestor worship** – 祭祖  
**memorial stele** – 纪念碑

## Writing practice  写作小练习

**根据我们这一节所学到的内容，写出下面句子的英文。**

1. 在清明节，人们会前往墓地扫墓，表达对先人的敬意。

   _____

2. 清明节的时候，人们会进行踏青郊游，感受大自然的魅力。

   _____

3. 人们在清明节放风筝，庆祝春天的到来。

   _____

## Reference translation 参考译文

清明节通常在4月初,这是中国的一个特殊节日。这一天,家人们通过扫墓祭祖来缅怀先人。

清明节对应着中国传统节气"清明",这个节气标志着春季的深入和万物复苏。在这个时候,天气渐暖,草木繁茂,是最适合出行和缅怀祖先的时候。

在清明节这一天,家家户户都会打扫墓地,并在墓上放上鲜花、食物和纸钱,以此来表达对先人的怀念和尊敬。这种习俗在中国有着悠久的历史,体现了家庭对历史和生命的重视。

除了扫墓,人们还喜欢外出亲近自然。春天是大自然复苏、万物生长的季节,人们会带着家人到郊外走走,享受大自然的美景,这也象征着对生命的庆祝和对新的一年的期待。

清明也是放风筝的好时节。在一些地方,尤其是在北方,家庭会一起放风筝。有的风筝上还会挂上小铃铛,当风筝在空中飘飞时,铃铛清脆的声音格外悦耳。人们相信这样可以把厄运和不幸"吹"走,带来健康和平安。

清明节不仅是纪念过去的一种方式,它也帮助人们欣赏现在的美好时光,并期待未来。通过这些传统的活动,清明节让每个人都能感受到家庭的温暖和春天的希望。

# The Dragon Boat Festival
端午节：一起来赛龙舟吧

**Listening & practice** 听英文原声，完成练习

1. When is the Dragon Boat Festival celebrated?
    A. On the fifth day of the fifth month in the Chinese lunar calendar
    B. On the first day of the first month in the Chinese lunar calendar
    C. On the tenth day of the tenth month in the Chinese lunar calendar

2. Who do people remember during the Dragon Boat Festival?
    A. Confucius
    B. Qu Yuan
    C. Li Bai

3. What special food do people eat during the Dragon Boat Festival?
    A. Dumplings
    B. Mooncakes
    C. Zongzi

4. Why do people race dragon boats during the festival?
    A. To find Qu Yuan and keep fish away
    B. To celebrate the New Year
    C. To have a party

5. What do people hang in their homes during the Dragon Boat Festival?
    A. Red lanterns
    B. Mugwort
    C. Flowers

## Reading 阅读下面的文章

The Dragon Boat Festival is one of China's traditional festivals celebrated on the fifth day of the fifth month in the Chinese lunar calendar every year. This festival is full of colours and activities, making it fun and **culturally** significant.

The history of the Dragon Boat Festival goes way back and started as a way to commemorate the ancient poet Qu Yuan. Qu Yuan was a **minister** in the kingdom of Chu and a great **patriotic** poet. Because he was so sad about the problems in his country, he **drowned** himself after being exiled. To keep fish from eating his body, people **paddled** dragon boats to search for him and threw rice **wrapped** in leaves into the river so the fish would eat that instead of him.

Since then, racing dragon boats and eating zongzi have become the main customs of the Dragon Boat Festival. Dragon boat races are very exciting. Everyone in the boat rows as hard as they can, hoping their boat will win.

Zongzi is a special food for the festival. It's sticky rice wrapped in bamboo leaves, sometimes filled with sweet or savory fillings, and shaped like a **triangle** or **rectangle**. It's really tasty.

Besides eating zongzi and racing dragon boats, people hang mugwort in their homes to keep away evil and bring good health to their families. In some places, people also wear colourful **threads** and drink realgar wine as part of the festival traditions.

The Dragon Boat Festival is not just about remembering Qu Yuan, but also shows people's love for life and their hopes for the future. It's a festival about **courage**, strength, and **protection**. Every celebration is filled with a longing for a good life and love for family.

## Vocabulary and phrases 词汇和短语

culturally [ˈkʌltʃərəli] 副 文化地

patriotic [ˌpeɪtriˈɒtɪk] 形 爱国的

paddle [ˈpædl] 动 划桨

triangle [ˈtraɪæŋgl] 名 三角形

thread [θred] 名 线；绳

protection [prəˈtekʃn] 名 保护；守卫

minister [ˈmɪnɪstə(r)] 名 大臣

drown [draʊn] 动 淹死

wrap [ræp] 动 包；裹

rectangle [ˈrektæŋgl] 名 长方形

courage [ˈkʌrɪdʒ] 名 勇气；胆量

## Practice 请选择合适的词填在下方的横线上

courage    protection    paddling    wrapped    threads

1. People threw zongzi into the river to offer _____ against the fish from eating Qu Yuan's body.

2. The sticky rice and prepared fillings are _____ in bamboo leaves.

3. People commemorate Qu Yuan by _____ dragon boats on this day, trying to find his body in the river.

4. Children wear these colourful _____ on their wrists, ankles, or necks to pray for health and happiness.

5. The Dragon Boat Festival is not only a holiday to commemorate Qu Yuan, but also a holiday to inherit the spirit of _____ and perseverance.

## Talking practice 情景对话模拟练习

端午节到了,郭鹏请他的外国朋友大卫品尝粽子,两个人展开了一段有趣的对话。

David大卫

Guo Peng, these zongzi are really tasty! What are they for?
郭鹏,这些粽子真好吃!它们是为了什么而做的?

Guo Peng郭鹏

They are for the Dragon Boat Festival, which is celebrated on the fifth day of the fifth lunar month.
它们是为了端午节做的,端午节在农历五月初五庆祝。

David大卫

Why do you eat zongzi on this day?
为什么你们在这一天吃粽子?

Guo Peng郭鹏

We eat zongzi to commemorate Qu Yuan, a great poet who drowned himself in a river.
我们吃粽子是为了纪念屈原,一位投江自尽的伟大诗人。

David大卫

What else do you do during the festival?
在节日期间你们还做什么?

Guo Peng郭鹏

We race dragon boats. It's very exciting, and everyone rows as fast as they can.
我们赛龙舟,非常激动人心,大家尽力划船。

David大卫

Do you have any other traditions?
你们还有其他传统吗?

Guo Peng郭鹏

Yes, we hang mugwort in our homes to keep away evil and bring good health.
有的,我们在家里挂艾草来祛邪保健。

## Funny facts  关于端午节的有趣事实和短语

佩香囊：端午节期间，有的地方的人们会佩戴香囊，内装香草草药，有驱虫防病的功效，同时也增添节日气氛。

药浴：端午节有用草药煮水洗澡的传统，人们认为这样可以防病治病。

| | |
|---|---|
| **herbal sachet** – 香囊 | **sticky rice** – 糯米 |
| **five-colour threads** – 五彩绳 | **Miluo River** – 汨罗江 |
| **realgar wine** – 雄黄酒 | **calamus and mugwort** – 菖蒲与艾草 |

## Writing practice  写作小练习

根据我们这一节所学到的内容，写出下面句子的英文。

1. 在端午节这一天，人们会举行划龙舟比赛庆祝这个节日。

2. 粽子是端午节的传统美食，它是由糯米制成的。

3. 端午节是为了纪念中国的一位爱国诗人屈原。

## Reference translation 参考译文

端午节是中国的传统节日之一，每年农历五月初五庆祝。这个节日丰富多彩，活动多样，既有趣又有深厚的文化意义。

端午节的历史非常悠久，最初是为了纪念古代诗人屈原。屈原是楚国的大臣，也是一位伟大的爱国诗人。由于他对国家的困境深感痛心，在被流放后投江自尽。人们为了阻止鱼吃掉他的身体，便划起龙舟出江寻找，并将用叶子包裹的米饭投入江中，希望鱼吃这些米饭而不吃他的身体。

自那以后，赛龙舟和吃粽子成为了端午节的主要习俗。龙舟赛非常激动人心，船上的每个人都拼尽全力划桨，希望自己的船能够获胜。

粽子是端午节的特色美食，它是用竹叶包裹的糯米，有时里面会加入甜或咸的馅料，形状多为三角形或长方形，很是美味。

除了吃粽子和赛龙舟，人们还会在家中挂起艾草，为了祛邪避疫，保佑家人平安健康。在一些地区，人们还会佩戴彩色丝线，饮用雄黄酒，作为节日传统的一部分。

端午节不仅仅是为了纪念屈原，也表达了人们对生活的热爱和对未来的美好祝愿。它是一个关于勇气、力量和保护的节日，每个庆祝活动都充满了对美好生活的向往和对家人的爱。

# The Mid-Autumn Festival
中秋节：每逢佳节倍思亲

**Listening & practice** 听英文原声，完成练习

▶扫码听音频◀

1. **When is the Mid-Autumn Festival celebrated?**
   A. On the first day of the first month in Chinese lunar calendar
   B. On the tenth day of the tenth month in Chinese lunar calendar
   C. On the fifteenth day of the eighth month in Chinese lunar calendar

2. **What special food do people eat during the Mid-Autumn Festival?**
   A. Dumplings
   B. Mooncakes
   C. Zongzi

3. **Why do people eat mooncakes during the Mid-Autumn Festival?**
   A. They are easy to make
   B. They are good for health
   C. They mean being complete and together

4. **What do people write on sky lanterns?**
   A. Wishes
   B. Names
   C. Riddles

5. **Why do people enjoy looking at the moon during the Mid-Autumn Festival?**
   A. To see the stars
   B. To feel close with family and friends
   C. To find the North Star

## Reading 阅读下面的文章

The Mid-Autumn Festival, also known as the August Festival, is a special celebration in China. It happens every year on the fifteenth day of the eighth month in Chinese lunar calendar. On this day, the moon looks very round, and this **roundness** means everyone being together and happy, so it's a time when families come together.

This festival started a very long time ago. Even before the Qin Dynasty, people in China had a tradition of celebrating the moon in the fall. By the time of the Tang Dynasty, it became an **official** holiday. On this day, both the emperor and regular people would admire the full moon and eat **mooncakes** to celebrate.

Mooncakes are a special treat for this festival. They are round cakes with different fillings like sweet bean paste or nuts. Mooncakes are **yummy**, and their round shape stands for being complete and together.

Besides eating mooncakes, another fun thing people do during this festival is **release** sky lanterns. People write wishes on the lanterns and let them **float** up into the sky, hoping their wishes will come true.

People also enjoy admiring the full moon. Families and friends gather to see the **bright**, full moon and share stories and **snacks**. This is more than just enjoying the beautiful view of the moon; it's about feeling close and warm with family.

Today, not just in China but in Chinese **communities** all over the world, people celebrate the Mid-Autumn Festival. It's a time to be **thankful** for the harvest and to enjoy the moon, but it's also about showing love to family and friends. These traditions help everyone feel good about the future and show how much they care for each other.

Every year on the night of the Mid-Autumn Festival, no matter where people are, they think about their loved ones and the bright moon brings their wishes and blessings together.

## Vocabulary and phrases 词汇和短语

roundness [raʊndnəs] 名 圆

mooncake [ˈmuːnkeɪk] 名 月饼

release [rɪˈliːs] 动 释放

bright [braɪt] 形 明亮的

community [kəˈmjuːnəti] 名 社区

official [əˈfɪʃl] 形 官方的；正式的

yummy [ˈjʌmi] 形 美味的；好吃的

float [fləʊt] 动 漂浮

snack [snæk] 名 小吃；点心

thankful [ˈθæŋkfl] 形 感谢的；感激的

## Practice 请选择合适的词填在下方的横线上

snacks　Mooncakes　float　bright　thankful

1. Families gather together to admire the _____ full moon, expressing their aspirations for a better life.

2. _____ are the traditional food of the Mid-Autumn Festival, symbolizing reunion and happiness.

3. This encourages us to be _____ for the world we live in and the opportunities we have.

4. Sky lanterns are made of paper with a candle inside that can_____ into the sky.

5. On this special day, people will eat mooncakes and various delicious _____ together.

## Talking practice 情景对话模拟练习

米歇尔和王婷聊起了中国的传统节日,王婷向她介绍了中秋节的风俗习惯。

Wang Ting, is there any traditional festival in China during the autumn?
王婷,秋天中国有传统节日吗?

Michelle米歇尔

Wang Ting王婷

Yes, we have the Mid-Autumn Festival. It's a special celebration on the fifteenth day of the eighth lunar month.
有的,我们有中秋节。这是在农历八月十五的特别庆祝活动。

Why is this festival important?
这个节日为什么重要?

Michelle米歇尔

Wang Ting王婷

It's a time for families to come together and enjoy the full moon, which stands for happiness and togetherness.
这是家人团聚的时刻,享受满月,象征着幸福和团圆。

What special food do you eat during the festival?
在节日期间你们吃什么特别的食物?

Michelle米歇尔

Wang Ting王婷

We eat mooncakes. They are round cakes with sweet fillings like bean paste or nuts.
我们吃月饼。它们是圆形的糕点,里面有甜的豆沙或坚果馅。

What other activities do you do?
你们还有什么活动?

Michelle米歇尔

Wang Ting王婷

We release sky lanterns with wishes written on them and enjoy the bright, full moon with family and friends.
我们放天灯,上面写着愿望,还和家人朋友一起欣赏明亮的满月。

## Funny facts  关于中秋节的有趣事实和短语

兔儿爷：兔儿爷是中秋节的一种民间玩具，源于嫦娥奔月的传说。据说玉兔陪伴嫦娥在月宫，成为月亮的象征之一。

提花灯：中秋节有提花灯的习俗，特别是在南方地区。花灯形状多样，有兔子灯、莲花灯、鱼灯等，小孩子们提着花灯玩耍，增加了节日的趣味。

文人雅集：历史上，中秋节也是文人墨客相聚吟诗作赋、饮酒赏月的时刻。许多名篇佳作如苏轼的《水调歌头·明月几时有》就是在中秋节创作的。

Chang'e – 嫦娥
jade rabbit – 玉兔
lotus paste – 莲蓉
salted egg yolk – 咸蛋黄

five-kernel – 五仁
full moon – 满月
rabbit lantern – 兔子灯

## Writing practice  写作小练习

**根据我们这一节所学到的内容，写出下面句子的英文。**

1. 中秋节是一个全家人团聚的节日。

2. 人们喜欢在中秋节的时候一边赏月，一边品尝月饼。

3. 月饼是中秋节的传统食物，它非常美味。

## Reference translation 参考译文

中秋节,又被称为八月节,是中国传统的节日之一,每年农历八月十五庆祝。这一天月亮特别圆,这种圆形象征着团圆和满足,因此,中秋节也是一个家人团聚的节日。

这个节日的历史非常悠久。甚至在秦朝之前,中国人就有在秋天祭月的习俗。到了唐朝,中秋节已经成为正式的节日。这一天,皇帝和百姓都会一起赏月和吃月饼来庆祝中秋节。

月饼是这个节日的特色美食。它们是圆形的糕点,有不同的馅料,如甜豆沙或坚果。月饼非常美味,它们的圆形代表着完美和团聚。

除了吃月饼,人们在节日期间还会做另一件有趣的事情,那就是放飞天灯。人们在天灯上写下愿望,让它们飘向天空,希望愿望能够实现。

人们还喜欢赏月。家人和朋友会聚在一起,观看明亮的满月,分享彼此的故事和美食。这个习俗不仅仅是欣赏月亮的美丽,更是一种享受家庭亲密和温暖的方式。

如今,不仅在中国,在世界各地的华人社区,人们都会庆祝中秋节。这是一个感恩收获和赏月的时候,也是向家人和朋友表达爱意的时刻。这些传统让每个人都对未来充满期待,并展现了他们彼此之间的深厚情感。

每年中秋之夜,无论人们身在何处,都会思念自己的亲人,而那轮明亮的月亮则将他们的愿望和祝福汇聚在一起。

# Twenty-four Solar Terms
## 二十四节气：中国古代智慧结晶

**Listening & practice** 听英文原声，完成练习

▶扫码听音频◀

1. How old is the "Twenty-four Solar Terms"?
   A. Over 500 years old
   B. Over 1,000 years old
   C. Over 2,000 years old

2. How many seasons are in the "Twenty-four Solar Terms"?
   A. Two
   B. Four
   C. Six

3. What do farmers use the solar terms for?
   A. To decide when to watch TV
   B. To decide when to plant, grow, harvest, and store crops
   C. To decide when to travel

4. What do people eat on the "Beginning of Spring" day (立春)?
   A. Spring rolls or pancakes
   B. Dumplings
   C. Mooncakes

5. What does the "Twenty-four Solar Terms" show about Chinese people?
   A. They like to play games
   B. They work well with nature and use their knowledge
   C. They travel a lot

## Reading 阅读下面的文章

China's "Twenty-four Solar Terms" is a special calendar that helps with farming and daily life. It started over 2,000 years ago near the Yellow River in China and shows ancient Chinese wisdom.

These twenty-four solar terms are split into four seasons—spring, summer, autumn, and winter. Each season has six terms that tell about the changes in nature and how crops grow during the year.

The solar terms can help farmers plan their farming activities. Farmers use these terms to decide when to plant, irrigate, harvest, and store their crops. Doing these activities at the right times helps them get a lot of food from their farms.

The solar terms also affect how Chinese people live every day. Each term has its own special customs. For example, on the "Beginning of Spring" day, people eat spring rolls or spring pancakes to celebrate spring's arrival. During the "Pure Brightness" term, people visit graves to remember their family members who have died.

The solar terms show how Chinese people work well with nature and use their knowledge to make the most of it. By learning about these terms,

we can enjoy how the seasons **change**, understand nature better, and learn a lot about farming and living.

The Twenty-four Solar Terms are not just a farming calendar. They are a big part of Chinese culture and traditions and **affect** how people live, even today.

## Vocabulary and phrases 词汇和短语

solar ['səʊlə(r)] 形 太阳的

split [splɪt] 动 将……分成若干部分

crop [krɒp] 名 农作物；庄稼

custom ['kʌstəm] 名 习惯；风俗

change [tʃeɪndʒ] 动 变化；改变

farming ['fɑːmɪŋ] 名 农业

season ['siːzn] 名 季节

store [stɔː(r)] 动 贮藏

pancake ['pænkeɪk] 名 薄煎饼

affect [ə'fekt] 动 影响

## Practice 请选择合适的词填在下方的横线上

Solar    farming    customs    store    affects

1. Each solar term has its unique _____ and habits.

2. Twenty-four _____ Terms can guide our production and life.

3. Twenty-four Solar Terms have served as a valuable guide for _____ practices in China.

4. The changing of seasons significantly _____ the optimal times for planting and harvesting of crops.

5. After harvest we _____ the grain.

## Talking practice　情景对话模拟练习

杰克在向赵雪询问中国传统二十节气的知识，你也一起来模拟这段对话吧。

I heard that China has a traditional calendar with twenty-four solar terms. Is that true?
我听说中国有个传统的二十四节气，是这样吗？

Jack杰克

Zhao Xue赵雪
Yes, that's true. The Twenty-four Solar Terms help with farming and daily life.
是的，没错。二十四节气有助于农业和日常生活。

When did this calendar start?
这个日历是什么时候开始的？

Jack杰克

Zhao Xue赵雪
It started over 2,000 years ago near the Yellow River in China.
它始于2,000多年前的中国黄河附近。

How do farmers use the solar terms?
农民们如何使用这些节气？

Jack杰克

Zhao Xue赵雪
Farmers use them to decide when to plant, irrigate, harvest, and store their crops.
农民们用它们来决定何时种植、灌溉、收获和储存作物。

Are there any special customs for these terms?
这些节气有特别的习俗吗？

Jack杰克

Zhao Xue 赵雪

Yes, each term has special customs. For example, during the "Beginning of Spring", people eat spring rolls to celebrate.
有的，每个节气都有特别的习俗。例如，在"立春"时，人们吃春卷来庆祝。

Wow, that sounds really interesting!
哇，听起来真的很有趣！

Jack 杰克

## Funny facts  关于二十四节气的有趣事实和短语

**农事指导**：二十四节气为古代农民提供了重要的农业生产指导，如春耕、夏种、秋收、冬藏。每个节气都有特定的农事活动和习俗。

**民间谚语**：关于二十四节气的谚语广泛流传，如"春雨惊春清谷天，夏满芒夏暑相连，秋处露秋寒霜降，冬雪雪冬小大寒"等，形象地总结了各节气的气候特点和农事活动。

**世界遗产**：2016年，二十四节气被联合国教科文组织列入人类非物质文化遗产代表作名录，标志着其在全球文化遗产中的重要地位。

- Beginning of Spring – 立春
- Rain Water – 雨水
- Waking of Insects – 惊蛰
- Spring Equinox – 春分
- Pure Brightness – 清明
- Grain Rain – 谷雨
- Beginning of Summer – 立夏
- Grain Full – 小满
- Grain in Ear – 芒种
- Summer Solstice – 夏至
- Slight Heat – 小暑
- Great Heat – 大暑
- Beginning of Autumn – 立秋
- Limit of Heat – 处暑
- White Dew – 白露
- Autumn Equinox – 秋分
- Cold Dew – 寒露
- Frost's Descent – 霜降
- Beginning of Winter – 立冬
- Slight Snow – 小雪
- Great Snow – 大雪
- Winter Solstice – 冬至
- Slight Cold – 小寒
- Great Cold – 大寒

## Writing practice 写作小练习

**根据我们这一节所学到的内容，写出下面句子的英文。**

1. 二十四节气产生在中国的黄河附近。

   _____

2. 节气可以帮助农民安排农事活动。

   _____

3. 立春的时候，人们喜欢吃春饼。

   _____

## Reference translation 参考译文

　　中国的"二十四节气"是一部独特的历法，它承载着农耕与生活的智慧。这一传统可以追溯到2,000多年前的黄河流域，是中国古代智慧的结晶。

　　二十四节气分为春、夏、秋、冬四季。每个季节包含六个节气，它们描述了一年中自然界的变化和农作物的生长周期。

　　根据二十四节气，农民可以更好地安排农事活动。农民们按照节气变化进行重要农事活动，包括何时播种，何时灌溉，何时收获，何时贮藏。这些活动确保了作物能在最佳时机种植和收获，从而保证食物的丰收。

　　二十四节气也深深影响了中国人的日常生活。每个节气都有其独特的风俗习惯。例如，在立春那天，人们会吃春卷或春饼来庆祝春天的到来。清明时节，人们则会去扫墓，缅怀先祖。

　　二十四节气不仅体现了中国人与自然的和谐相处，还展示了中国古人利用自然的智慧。通过了解和学习二十四节气，我们可以更好地欣赏季节的变化美，理解自然规律，同时也能学到很多关于耕种和生活的知识。

　　二十四节气不仅仅是一部农耕历法，它更是中华文化的重要组成部分，影响着人们的生活方式，直到今天。

# Part 4
# 中国的现代科技和文化

# China Railway Highspeed
## 中国高铁：有趣又快速的出行体验

**Listening & practice**  听英文原声，完成练习

▶扫码听音频◀

1. What do high-speed trains in China use for power?
   A. Electricity
   B. Diesel fuel
   C. Solar power

2. How fast can high-speed trains in China travel?
   A. 150 kilometres per hour
   B. 250 kilometres per hour
   C. 350 kilometres per hour

3. How long does it take to travel from Beijing to Shanghai by high-speed train?
   A. About 10 hours
   B. About 4.5 hours
   C. About 7 hours

4. What is one of the benefits of traveling by high-speed train?
   A. Free snacks
   B. Free Wi-Fi on many trains
   C. Free souvenirs

5. Why are high-speed trains good for the environment?
   A. They use electricity and produce less pollution
   B. They run on diesel fuel
   C. They are made of recycled materials

## Reading  阅读下面的文章

China railway highspeed, or "gaotie" in Chinese, is a modern marvel in China. These sleek and speedy trains can travel at **incredible** speeds, making them a popular way to get around the country. Let's learn more about China's high-speed trains and why they are so amazing!

High-speed trains in China can travel at speeds of up to 350 kilometres per hour. This means you can travel from one city to another in just a few hours! For example, a trip from Beijing to Shanghai, which used to take more than 10 hours by regular train, now takes only about 4.5 hours by high-speed train.

One of the best things about traveling by high-speed train is how **comfortable** it is. The seats are **spacious** and can recline, and there is **plenty of** legroom. There are also power outlets for charging your devices and free Wi-Fi on many trains. You can enjoy a smooth and quiet ride while looking out the window at the beautiful **scenery** passing by.

High-speed trains are also very safe and reliable. They run on special tracks that are designed to handle their high speeds, and there are many safety measures in place to **ensure** a smooth journey. Trains are almost always on time, so you can plan your trip without **worrying about** delays.

Traveling by high-speed train is also good for the **environment**. These trains use **electricity** instead of diesel fuel, which means they produce less pollution. By choosing high-speed trains, you are helping to keep the air clean and protect our planet.

Today, many people in China love to travel by high-speed train. It's a favourite choice for both business trips and **vacations**. Whether going to visit family, exploring new cities, or just enjoying a day trip, high-speed trains make travel easy and enjoyable. The **convenience** and efficiency of high-speed trains have made them an essential part of modern life in China.

## Vocabulary and phrases 词汇和短语

**incredible** [ɪnˈkredəbl] 形 难以置信的；惊人的

**spacious** [ˈspeɪʃəs] 形 宽敞的

**scenery** [ˈsiːnəri] 名 风景

**worry about** 短 担心

**electricity** [ɪˌlekˈtrɪsəti] 名 电

**convenience** [kənˈviːnjəns] 名 便利；舒适

**comfortable** [ˈkʌmftəbl] 形 舒适的

**plenty of** 短 很多的

**ensure** [ɪnˈʃʊə(r)] 动 保证；确保

**environment** [ɪnˈvaɪrənmənt] 名 环境

**vacation** [vəˈkeɪʃn] 名 假期

## Practice 请选择合适的词填在下方的横线上

scenery　　ensures　　worry about　　convenience　　electricity

1. Compared to planes, you don't have to _____ flight delays.

2. High-speed trains work by using _____ from overhead wires.

3. You can enjoy the _____ outside the window as you travel.

4. It has a very powerful control system that _____ the train running smoothly on the tracks.

5. It brings _____ and efficiency to travel, especially for long distances.

## Talking practice 情景对话模拟练习

埃文第一次乘坐中国的高铁，同学李勇询问起他的感受，让我们一起来模拟这段对话吧。

Li Yong 李勇

Evan, how do you feel about traveling by high-speed train?
埃文，你觉得乘坐高铁是一种怎样的体验？

Evan 埃文

I think it's amazing! The trains are so fast and comfortable.
我觉得太棒了！火车又快又舒服。

Li Yong 李勇

Yes, they can travel up to 350 kilometres per hour. It's very convenient.
是的，它们可以跑到每小时350公里。非常方便。

Evan 埃文

I love the seats. They are spacious and can recline. Plus, there's free Wi-Fi!
我喜欢座位。它们很宽敞，还可以倾斜。而且还有免费Wi-Fi！

Li Yong 李勇

And they are very safe and almost always on time.
而且它们非常安全，几乎总是准时。

Evan 埃文

That's great! I also heard that high-speed trains are good for the environment.
那太好了！我还听说高铁对环境有好处。

Li Yong 李勇

Yes, they use electricity and produce less pollution than diesel trains.
是的，它们使用电力，比柴油火车产生的污染少。

Evan 埃文

I really enjoy the smooth and quiet ride. It's a fantastic way to travel.
我真的很享受这种平稳安静的旅程。这是旅行的绝佳方式。

## Funny facts  关于中国高铁的有趣事实和短语

**全球最长**：中国拥有世界上最长的高铁网络，总里程超过45,000公里，连接全国众多城市和地区。

**世界最快**：中国的复兴号高铁是目前世界上最快的常规运营列车之一，最高时速可达350公里左右。

**安全纪录**：中国高铁自运营以来，保持了极高的安全纪录，严格的管理和先进的技术保障了高铁运行的安全性。

**China Railway Highspeed** – 中国高速铁路
**bullet train** – 动车组
**Fuxing (Rejuvenation) Train** – 复兴号
**Harmony Train** – 和谐号
**high-speed rail network** – 高铁网络
**railway station** – 火车站
**ticket booking** – 购票
**train attendant** – 列车员
**safety record** – 安全纪录

## Writing practice  写作小练习

根据我们这一节所学到的内容，写出下面句子的英文。

1. 高铁能以极高的速度行驶。

2. 高铁不仅宽敞，而且很舒服。

3. 从北京到上海，乘坐高铁只需要4.5小时。

## Reference translation 参考译文

中国高速铁路,即中文中的"高铁",堪称现代奇迹。这些流线型且快速的列车能够以惊人的速度行驶,使其成为在全国范围内出行的热门方式。让我们一起来了解中国的高铁,看看为什么它们如此令人惊叹!

中国的高铁列车速度可达每小时350公里。这意味着你可以在几个小时内从一个城市旅行到另一个城市!例如,从北京到上海的旅行,以前普通列车需要超过10小时,现在乘坐高铁只需约4.5小时。

乘坐高铁的一个最大优点是它的舒适性。座椅宽敞且可以倾斜,有足够的腿部空间。许多列车上还有电源插座用于给设备充电,并提供免费Wi-Fi。你可以在平稳而安静的旅程中欣赏窗外美丽的风景。

高铁也非常安全可靠。它们运行在专门设计的高铁轨道上,这些轨道能够承受高速行驶,并且有许多安全措施确保旅程的顺利进行。列车几乎总是准时到达,因此你可以放心安排旅行而不必担心延误。

乘坐高铁对环境也有好处。这些列车使用电力而不是柴油,这意味着它们产生的污染较少。选择高铁出行有助于保持空气清洁,保护我们的地球。

今天,许多中国人非常乐于乘坐高铁出行。无论是商务出差还是休闲度假,高铁都是一个备受欢迎的选择。无论是探亲访友,还是探索新城市,甚至只是享受一天的短途旅行,高铁都让旅行变得轻松愉快。高铁的便利和高效已成为中国现代生活中不可或缺的一部分。

# China's Space Exploration
## 中国的太空探索：追寻星辰大海

**Listening & practice** 听英文原声，完成练习

1. When did China launch its first satellite, Dongfanghong 1?
   A. 1960
   B. 1970
   C. 1980

2. Who was the first Chinese taikonaut sent into space?
   A. Liu Yang
   B. Jing Haipeng
   C. Yang Liwei

3. What is the name of China's space station?
   A. Tiangong
   B. Tianzhou
   C. Chang'e

4. What special achievement did the Chang'e 4 lunar probe accomplish?
   A. Landed on Mars
   B. Landed on the far side of the moon
   C. Flew to Jupiter

5. What inspires many young people in China to study STEM?
   A. Playing video games
   B. Watching TV shows
   C. China's space program

扫码听音频

## Reading   阅读下面的文章

China's space program is very exciting and impressive. From **launching** satellites to sending **astronauts** into space, China has done many amazing things. Let's learn more about China's space program and why it's so special!

China's journey into space began in 1970 with the launch of its first **satellite**, Dongfanghong 1. Since then, China has launched many satellites that help with weather forecasting, communication, and navigation.

One of the most amazing achievements of China's space program is sending taikonauts into space. In 2003, China sent its first taikonaut, Yang Liwei, into space on the Shenzhou V **spacecraft**. This made China the third country in the world to send a person into space by itself. Since then, China has continued to send taikonauts on many missions, including building the Tiangong space station.

The Tiangong space station, which means "Heavenly Palace", is a big step in China's space **exploration**. It is a place where taikonauts live and work, doing experiments and making new **discoveries**. It also helps prepare for future space missions.

China is also exploring the moon and beyond. In 2019, China made history by landing the lunar probe Chang'e-4 on the far side of the moon, a first for any country. The lunar probe, named after the Chinese moon goddess Chang'e, studies the moon's **surface** and collects important information.

China's space **achievements** make the country very proud. They show China's progress in **technology** and its determination to **explore** space. The space program also **inspires** many young people in China to study science, technology, engineering, and maths (STEM). From launching satellites to building space stations and exploring the moon, China is reaching for the stars and helping us learn more about the **universe**.

## Vocabulary and phrases 词汇和短语

launch [lɔːntʃ] 动 发射

satellite ['sætəlaɪt] 名 卫星；人造卫星

exploration [ˌekspləˈreɪʃn] 名 探索

surface ['sɜːfɪs] 名 表面

technology [tekˈnɒlədʒi] 名 技术

inspire [ɪnˈspaɪə(r)] 动 激励；鼓舞

taikonaut [ˈtaɪkənɔːt] 名 航天员

spacecraft [ˈspeɪskrɑːft] 名 宇宙飞船

discovery [dɪˈskʌvəri] 名 发现

achievement [əˈtʃiːvmənt] 名 成就；成绩

explore [ɪkˈsplɔː(r)] 动 探索

universe [ˈjuːnɪvɜːs] 名 宇宙

## Practice 请选择合适的词填在下方的横线上

launched   satellite   taikonauts   universe   surface

1. The _____ work and live in the space station.
2. China has successfully _____ many satellites.
3. They also hope to fly to distant planets in the future to explore the mysteries of the _____.
4. Our Chang'e lunar probe successfully left its footprints on the moon _____.
5. Dongfanghong 1 is China's first man-made _____ .

## Talking practice 情景对话模拟练习

说到中国的航天文化，大卫和吴迪正在热烈的讨论，你也跟着练习这段对话吧。

Wu Di, can you tell me about China's space program? It sounds very exciting!
吴迪，你能告诉我一些关于中国航天计划的事情吗？听起来很激动人心！

David大卫

Wu Di吴迪

Sure! China's space program started in 1970 with the launch of its first satellite, Dongfanghong 1.
当然可以！中国的航天计划始于1970年发射的第一颗卫星东方红一号。

That's amazing! Has China sent taikonauts into space?
那真了不起！中国有送航天员上太空吗？

David大卫

Wu Di吴迪

Yes, in 2003, China sent its first taikonaut, Yang Liwei, into space on the Shenzhou V spacecraft.
有的，2003年，中国把第一位航天员杨利伟送上了神舟五号飞船去探索太空。

What is the Tiangong space station?
天宫空间站是什么？

David大卫

Wu Di吴迪

The Tiangong space station, meaning "Heavenly Palace", is a place where taikonauts live and work in space.
天宫空间站，意思是"天宫"，是航天员在太空生活和工作的地方。

Has China explored the moon, too?
中国也探测过月球吗？

David大卫

中国的太空探索：追寻星辰大海　　159

Wu Di 吴迪

Yes, in 2019, China landed the lunar probe Chang'e 4 on the far side of the moon, which was a first for any country.
是的，2019年，中国将嫦娥四号月球探测器成功降落在月球背面，实现人类首次月背软着陆。

Wow, that's incredible! China's space program is really impressive.
哇，那真不可思议！中国的航天计划真的很令人印象深刻。

David 大卫

## Funny facts　关于中国太空探索的有趣事实和短语

**首次载人航天**：2003年10月15日，中国成功发射神舟五号飞船，杨利伟成为中国首位进入太空的航天员，中国成为世界上第三个独立掌握载人航天技术的国家。

**嫦娥计划**：嫦娥计划是中国的月球探测项目。嫦娥一号于2007年发射，成功进入月球轨道。2019年，嫦娥四号成功实现人类首次在月球背面软着陆。

**长征系列运载火箭**：长征系列火箭是中国主要的运载火箭，承担了大部分的航天发射任务。2020年5月，长征五号B运载火箭成功首飞，为天宫空间站的建设提供了强大运力支持。

- Shenzhou Spacecraft – 神舟飞船
- Chang'e Lunar Probe – 嫦娥探测器
- Long March Rockets – 长征火箭
- Zhurong Mars Rover – 祝融号火星车
- Yutu Lunar Rover – 玉兔号月球车
- Xichang Satellite Launch Centre – 西昌卫星发射中心
- Jiuquan Satellite Launch Centre – 酒泉卫星发射中心

## Writing practice　写作小练习

根据我们这一节所学到的内容，写出下面句子的英文。

1. 中国在太空探索上取得了伟大的成就。

2. 杨利伟是中国首位进入太空的航天员。

3. 建造更大的空间站,可以让更多航天员在太空中生活和工作。

## Reference translation 参考译文

中国的航天探索计划既激动人心又令人叹为观止。从发射卫星到送宇航员进入太空,中国完成了众多壮举。让我们一起来了解中国对太空的探索计划,看看为什么它们如此令人惊叹!

中国的太空之旅始于1970年,第一颗卫星"东方红一号"的升空。自此以后,中国发射了众多卫星,它们在天气预报、通信和导航等领域发挥着重要作用。

中国航天计划最引人注目的成就之一是载人航天任务。2003年,中国首次将乘坐神舟五号飞船的航天员杨利伟送入太空。中国成为世界上第三个独立将人类送入太空的国家。此后,中国继续进行多次载人任务,包括建设天宫空间站。

天宫空间站,意思是"天上的宫殿",是中国对太空探索的重要里程碑。这里是航天员生活与工作的场所,他们在此进行实验,不断取得新的发现。同时,天宫空间站也为未来的太空任务奠定了坚实基础。

中国也不断地探索月球及更远的地方。2019年,中国创造了历史,成功将嫦娥四号探测器着陆在月球背面,实现人类首次月背软着陆。探测器以中国的月亮女神嫦娥命名,其任务是研究月球表面并收集重要的科学信息。

中国的航天成就让整个国家倍感自豪,它们彰显了中国在科技领域的进步以及探索太空的坚定决心。航天计划还激发了中国众多年轻人对科学、技术、工程和数学(STEM)领域的追求。从发射卫星到建造空间站,再到探索月球,中国正一步步迈向星辰大海,引领我们更加深入地了解宇宙的奥秘。

# Digital Life in China
## 数字生活在中国：一种新的生活方式

### Listening & practice  听英文原声，完成练习

1. What has made daily life more convenient in China?
   A. Reading books
   B. Riding bicycles
   C. Digital technology

2. Which app is popular for watching short videos in China?
   A. Tmall
   B. WeChat Pay
   C. TikTok

3. How can you make payments in China using a smartphone?
   A. By sending a letter
   B. By scanning a QR code
   C. By using cash

4. What can you watch on streaming platforms like iQiyi and Tencent Video?
   A. Live sports only
   B. Movies and TV shows
   C. Weather forecasts

5. Which social media app helps people stay in touch with friends and family in China?
   A. WeChat
   B. TikTok
   C. Tmall

## Reading　阅读下面的文章

China's digital life has **transformed** daily routines, making everything more convenient and enjoyable. From online shopping and watching short videos to using **digital** payments, technology has become deeply embedded in everyday life. Let's explore how digital culture has **enriched** the lives of people in China!

One of the most popular parts of digital life in China is online shopping. With just a few clicks, you can buy anything you need and have it **delivered** to your door. Websites like Tmall and JD.com have millions of products, from clothes and toys to food and electronics. Online shopping saves time and makes it easy to find exactly what you want.

Watching short videos is another favourite digital activity in China. Apps like TikTok and RED let people create and watch short videos about everything you can imagine. From funny clips and dance **challenges** to cooking tips and travel adventures, there is something for everyone. Watching short videos is a fun way to relax and be entertained.

Digital **payments** have also made life in China much easier. With apps like Alipay and WeChat Pay, you can pay for anything using your **smartphone**. Whether you are buying groceries, paying for a taxi, or even giving money to a friend, digital payments are fast and safe. You don't need to carry cash or worry about losing your wallet. Everything is done with a simple scan of a QR code.

Digital life has also made entertainment more **diverse** and **accessible**. People can watch movies and TV shows on streaming platforms like iQiyi and Tencent Video. Online games are very popular too, with millions of people playing games like *Honor of Kings* and *Game of Peace*. Virtual concerts and live-streaming events are also common, bringing entertainment directly to people's homes.

**In addition to** making life more convenient and fun, digital life in China has connected people in new ways. Social media apps like WeChat and Micro Blog help people stay in touch with friends and family, share their **experiences**, and meet new people. These apps have become a big part of everyday life and culture in China.

Digital life in China is a wonderful example of how technology can improve our lives. It makes everything faster, easier, and more enjoyable. Whether you are shopping online, watching a funny video, or paying for a meal with your phone, digital life has something for everyone. It's a new way of living that has become an important part of modern Chinese culture.

## Vocabulary and phrases 词汇和短语

transform [træns'fɔːm] 动 改变；转换

enrich [ɪn'rɪtʃ] 动 使丰富；使富足

challenge ['tʃælɪndʒ] 名 挑战

smartphone ['smɑːtfəʊn] 名 智能手机

accessible [ək'sesəbl] 形 可得到的；易于获得的

experience [ɪk'spɪəriəns] 名 经历

digital ['dɪdʒɪtl] 形 数字的；数码的

deliver [dɪ'lɪvə(r)] 动 送货；交付

payment ['peɪmənt] 名 支付

diverse [daɪ'vɜːs] 形 不同的；多种多样的

in addition to 短 除……之外（还）

## Practice 请选择合适的词填在下方的横线上

deliver    smartphones    Digital    payment    transformed

1. _____ life makes communication more accessible.

2. Through electronic devices such as _____ and computers, we can stay in touch with friends and family anytime.

3. It has _____ the way we communicate, learn, and entertain ourselves.

4. We can use digital _____ without the need to carry cash or bank cards.

5. They promise to _____ to your door within 48 hours of you ordering.

## Talking practice 情景对话模拟练习

艾米在中国生活了一段时间，她把自己的感受告诉了好朋友张雪，让我们一起来跟着练习这段对话。

Zhang Xue, you know what? I found that living in China is really convenient!
张雪，你知道吗？我发现在中国生活实在是太方便了。

Amy艾米

Zhang Xue张雪
Yes, digital life has changed a lot. What do you find most convenient?
是的，数字生活改变了很多。你觉得什么最方便？

I love online shopping. I can buy anything I need with just a few clicks.
我喜欢网购。我只需点击几下就能买到任何需要的东西。

Amy艾米

Zhang Xue张雪
Me, too! Websites like Tmall and JD.com have so many products.
我也是！像天猫和京东这样的网站有很多商品。

I also enjoy watching short videos on TikTok. It's so entertaining!
我也喜欢在抖音上看短视频。真有趣！

Amy艾米

Zhang Xue 张雪

Yes, there are videos about everything, from cooking to travel.
是的，有关于各种事物的视频，从烹饪到旅行都有。

Amy 艾米

And digital payments are so easy. I use Alipay and WeChat Pay all the time.
而且数字支付很方便。我一直用支付宝和微信支付。

Zhang Xue 张雪

Exactly! You can pay for anything with your phone. It's fast and safe.
没错！你可以用手机支付任何东西。又快又安全。

## Funny facts  关于数字生活的有趣事实和短语

**移动支付普及**：中国是全球移动支付最普及的国家之一，支付宝和微信支付是最主要的两大移动支付平台。

**短视频热潮**：短视频平台如抖音、快手和小红书等在中国年轻人当中非常受欢迎。

| | |
|---|---|
| **online shopping** – 网络购物 | **online games** – 网络游戏 |
| **digital payments** – 数字支付 | **social media** – 社交媒体 |
| **short videos** – 短视频 | **live-streaming sale** – 直播销售 |

## Writing practice  写作小练习

根据我们这一节所学到的内容，写出下面句子的英文。

1. 我们可以随时随地进行网上购物。

_____

2. 在今天的生活中，数字支付又快又安全。

_____

3. 我们可以通过网络玩游戏、观看电影和听音乐。

## Reference translation 参考译文

中国的数字生活已悄然改变了人们的日常习惯，使一切变得更加便捷与愉悦。从网络购物、观看短视频到数字支付，科技已深深融入日常生活的每个角落。让我们一同探索数字文化如何丰富了中国人的生活！

网上购物是中国数字生活中最受欢迎的部分之一。只需点击几下，你就可以购买到你需要的任何东西并享受送货上门的服务。像天猫和京东这样的网站上有成千上万的商品，从衣服和玩具到食品和电子产品。网上购物节省时间，让你轻松找到自己想要的东西。

观看短视频则是另一项深受国人喜爱的数字活动。像抖音和小红书这样的应用程序让人们可以制作和观看各种短视频。从趣味短片、舞蹈挑战到烹饪秘籍、旅行奇遇，总有一款能触动你的心弦。看短视频是一种放松和娱乐的有趣方式。

数字支付也让中国的生活变得更加便捷。通过支付宝和微信支付等应用程序，你可以用手机支付任何东西。无论是购买杂货、支付出租车费，还是给朋友转账，数字支付都快捷且安全。你不需要携带现金，也不用担心丢钱包。一切都可以通过扫描二维码来完成。

数字生活还让娱乐变得更加多样化和易于获取。人们可以在爱奇艺和腾讯视频等流媒体平台上观看电影和电视剧。网络游戏也非常受欢迎，数百万人在玩《王者荣耀》和《和平精英》。虚拟演唱会和直播活动也很常见，将娱乐直接带到人们的家中。

除了让生活更加便捷和有趣，中国的数字生活还以全新的方式将人们紧密相连。像微信和微博这样的社交媒体应用帮助人们与朋友和家人保持联系，分享他们的经历，认识新朋友。这些应用已经成为中国日常生活和文化的一部分。

中国的数字生活是技术如何改善我们生活的一个绝佳例子。它使一切变得更快、更容易和更愉快。无论你是在网上购物、看搞笑视频，还是用手机支付餐费，数字生活总能为每个人带来独特的体验。这是一种新的生活方式，已经成为中国现代文化的重要组成部分。

# New Energy Vehicles
## 新能源汽车：驶向未来

**Listening & practice** 听英文原声，完成练习

▶扫码听音频◀

1. What is the most common type of NEV in China?

    A. Hydrogen fuel cell vehicles (氢能源汽车)

    B. Electric vehicles

    C. Hybrid electrical vehicles

2. Where can you charge an electric vehicles in China?

    A. At home

    B. At public charging stations

    C. Both A and B

3. What is a benefit of hybrid electrical vehicles?

    A. They are faster than electric vehicles

    B. They use both an electric motor and a gasoline engine

    C. They produce more emissions than traditional vehicles

4. What do hydrogen fuel cell vehicles produce as a byproduct?

    A. Carbon dioxide

    B. Water

    C. Methane

5. Why are NEVs important for the environment?

    A. They reduce reliance on fossil fuels

    B. They increase air pollution

    C. They use more gasoline

## Reading  阅读下面的文章

China is leading the way in the development and use of new energy **vehicles** ——NEVs. These include electric vehicles, hybrid electrical vehicles, hydrogen fuel cell vehicles... NEVs are becoming very popular in China, offering a cleaner, more **sustainable** way to travel.

Electric vehicles are the most common type of NEV in China. They run on electricity stored in **batteries**, which can be **charged** at home or at public charging stations. Popular models like Build Your Dreams (BYD), NIO, and LiAuto are seen more and more on the roads. Electric vehicles are not only better for the environment, producing no **emissions**, but they are also quieter and cheaper to run than traditional gasoline cars.

Charging an electric vehicle is becoming easier as well. China has built the largest network of charging stations in the world, with more being added every day. In big cities, you can find charging stations at shopping malls, office buildings, and even **residential** complexes. This makes owning an electric vehicle very convenient.

Hybrid electrical Vehicles, which use both an electric motor and a gasoline engine, are also popular. They offer the best of both worlds: the ability to drive longer distances without worrying about finding a charging station and the environmental benefits of reduced emissions. Chinese brands like BYD and Geely have produced some of the best hybrid electrical vehicles, earning praise for their quality and **innovation**.

Hydrogen fuel cell vehicles are another exciting development. These vehicles **generate** electricity through a chemical reaction between hydrogen and oxygen, producing only water as a byproduct. Although still in the early stages of development, hydrogen vehicles have the **potential** to offer even greater ranges and faster refueling times than electric vehicles.

NEVs are more than just a trend, they are part of a larger movement towards sustainability and environmental protection. By reducing reliance on fossil fuels, NEVs help to **decrease** air pollution and combat climate change.

If you have the chance to ride in or drive a new energy vehicle, you will see why they are so popular. They are smooth, quiet, and full of **advanced** technology. NEVs are driving China into a cleaner, greener future.

## Vocabulary and phrases 词汇和短语

vehicle ['viːɪkl] 名 交通工具；车辆

battery ['bætərɪ] 名 电池

emission [ɪ'mɪʃn] 名 排放物

innovation [ˌɪnə'veɪʃn] 名 创新；革新

potential [pə'tenʃl] 名 潜力；潜能

advanced [əd'vɑːnst] 形 先进的

sustainable [sə'steɪnəbl] 形 可持续的

charge [tʃɑːdʒ] 动 充电

residential [ˌrezɪ'denʃl] 形 住宅的；居住的

generate ['dʒenəreɪt] 动 产生；生产

decrease [dɪ'kriːs] 动 降低

## Practice 请选择合适的词填在下方的横线上

vehicle    battery    decrease    charge    advanced

1. NEVs integrate _____ technologies in vehicle power control and drive systems.

2. They can _____ harmful gases produced into the air.

3. When you drive the car, the _____ releases energy to power the motor.

4. Electric cars are a special kind of _____ that runs on electricity.

5. The development of the fast charging technology allows vehicles to _____ at higher speeds.

## Talking practice 情景对话模拟练习

丹尼尔来到中国没多久，兴致勃勃地和好友刘楠聊起了他的发现，你也来练习这段对话吧。

Daniel 丹尼尔

Liu Nan, I noticed there are many electric vehicles on the streets in China. They look so nice!
刘楠，我发现中国的大街上有很多电动汽车，它们都非常漂亮。

Liu Nan 刘楠

Yes, electric vehicles are very popular here. They are good for the environment because they don't produce emissions.
是的，电动汽车在这里非常受欢迎。它们对环境有好处，因为不产生尾气排放。

Daniel 丹尼尔

How do people charge their electric vehicles?
人们如何给电动汽车充电呢？

Liu Nan 刘楠

There are many charging stations in big cities, like at shopping malls and office buildings.
大城市有很多充电站，比如在购物中心和办公地点。

Daniel 丹尼尔

What about hybrid electrical vehicles? Are they also popular in China?
那混合动力汽车呢？它们在中国也很受欢迎吗？

Liu Nan 刘楠

Yes, hybrid electrical vehicles are popular, too. They use both electricity and gasoline, so you can drive longer distances.
是的，混合动力汽车也很受欢迎。它们既使用电力又使用汽油，所以你可以开更长的距离。

Daniel 丹尼尔

I've heard about hydrogen fuel cell vehicles. Are they used in China?
我听说过氢燃料电池车。它们在中国使用吗？

Liu Nan 刘楠

Yes, but they are still new. They produce only water as a byproduct and have great potential for the future.
是的，但它们还很新。它们只产生水作为副产品，并且在未来有很大的潜力。

That's amazing! It seems like China is really leading the way in new energy vehicles.
那真了不起！看起来中国在新能源车方面真的走在前列。

Daniel 丹尼尔

## Funny facts  关于新能源汽车的有趣事实和短语

**全球最大市场**：中国是全球最大的新能源汽车市场之一。

**新势力造车**：中国涌现了一批新的电动汽车制造商，如蔚来、小鹏和理想等，这些企业以智能化和高性能为卖点，迅速占领市场。

**自动驾驶**：中国的电动汽车制造商积极研发自动驾驶技术，百度、华为等科技公司也在推动自动驾驶技术的发展。

---

electric vehicle (EV) – 电动汽车
smart grid – 智能电网
autonomous driving – 自动驾驶
hybrid electrical vehicle (HEV) – 混合动力汽车

charging pile – 充电桩
zero emission – 零排放
battery recycling – 电池回收

---

## Writing practice  写作小练习

根据我们这一节所学到的内容，写出下面句子的英文。

1. 在中国，新能源汽车非常流行。

2. 新能源汽车可以减少空气污染，有利于环境。

3. 电动汽车不需要汽油，只需要充电。

---

## Reference translation 参考译文

中国正引领着新能源汽车（NEVs）——包括电动汽车、混合动力汽车、氢燃料电池汽车等——的研发与使用之路。这些新能源汽车正风靡中国，为出行提供了一种更加清洁、可持续的方式。

在中国，电动汽车是最常见的新能源汽车类型。它们依赖电池储存的电力运行，可以在家中或公共充电站充电。比亚迪（BYD）、蔚来和理想等热门车型正越来越多地出现在道路上。电动汽车不仅对环境更为友好，实现零排放，而且运行起来比传统汽油车更安静、更经济。

给电动汽车充电也变得越来越便捷。中国已经建成了世界上最大的充电站网络，每天都在增加更多的充电站。在大城市中，你可以在购物中心、办公楼、甚至住宅小区找到充电站。这使得拥有电动汽车非常方便。

混合动力汽车同样备受欢迎，它们兼具电动电机和汽油发动机的优势。混合动力汽车能够让你无需担心寻找充电站，轻松驾驶更远距离，同时又能享受减少排放带来的环保益处。比亚迪、吉利等中国品牌生产的混合动力汽车凭借其卓越的品质和创新赢得了广泛赞誉。

氢燃料电池汽车是另一个令人兴奋的发展方向。这些汽车通过氢气和氧气之间的化学反应发电，仅产生水作为副产品。尽管仍处于开发的早期阶段，氢燃料汽车有望提供比电动汽车更长的续驶里程和更快的加氢时间。

新能源汽车不仅仅是一个趋势，它们是朝着可持续性和环境保护迈进的一部分。通过减少对化石燃料的依赖，新能源汽车有助于减少空气污染和应对气候变化。

如果你有机会乘坐或驾驶新能源汽车，你会明白它们为什么如此受欢迎。它们运行平稳、安静，并充满了先进技术。新能源汽车正将中国驶向一个更加清洁、更加绿色的未来。

# Artificial Intelligence (AI)
## 人工智能：未来就在眼前

**Listening & practice** 听英文原声，完成练习

▶扫码听音频◀

1. What can smart robots do in hospitals in China?
   A. Teach students
   B. Drive cars
   C. Carry medicines and guide patients

2. What do self-driving cars use to drive themselves?
   A. Magic
   B. Artificial Intelligence (AI)
   C. Human drivers

3. What can AI assistants like Xiaodu and Tmall Genie help you with?
   A. Cooking dinner
   B. Doing your homework
   C. Traveling to space

4. How does AI make home life easier?
   A. By controlling lights and air conditioners
   B. By building houses
   C. By growing food

5. How is AI used in schools to help students?
   A. By teaching physical education classes
   B. By taking exams for students
   C. By giving instant feedback and personalized lessons

## Reading 阅读下面的文章

Have you ever **imagined** this: robots can help you with your housework, cars can drive themselves, and computers can understand and talk to you? This sounds like a scene from a sci-fi movie, but in China, these things are becoming real through **Artificial Intelligence**, AI.

AI is like a super-smart brain created by computers. It can learn, think, and solve problems just like humans. In China, AI is used in many exciting ways. For example, smart robots can help doctors in hospitals by carrying medicines and showing patients where to go. Some robots can even perform simple surgeries!

Self-driving cars are another amazing use of AI in China. These cars can drive by themselves without a human driver. They use AI to understand the road, follow traffic rules, and avoid **obstacles**. Technology companies like Huawei and Baidu are testing these cars on the streets, and soon they might become a common sight.

In China, there are also AI **assistants** like Xiaodu and Tmall Genie that can do many things. They can answer your questions, play your favourite music, tell you stories. These assistants are like friendly helpers that live in your **devices**.

AI is also making home life easier and more fun. Smart home devices can **control** lights, air conditioners, and even kitchen equipments. You can tell your smart speaker to turn off the lights, set the **temperature**, or start cooking dinner. It's like having a magic wand that makes things happen with your voice!

In schools, AI is used to make learning more interesting. Some AI learning apps help students **practice** maths, learn new words, and even study science. These apps give **instant** feedback and personalized lessons, making studying more fun and **effective**.

China's AI culture is a great example of how technology can improve our lives. It makes everything smarter, easier, and more fun. Whether it's robots in hospitals, self-driving cars, or smart home devices, AI is bringing the future to us today. Imagine all the exciting things AI will do in the future!

## Vocabulary and phrases 词汇和短语

imagine [ɪˈmædʒɪn] 动 想象

intelligence [ɪnˈtelɪdʒəns] 名 智能

assistant [əˈsɪstənt] 名 助手

control [kənˈtrəʊl] 动 控制

practice [ˈpræktɪs] 动 练习

effective [ɪˈfektɪv] 形 有效的

artificial [ˌɑːtɪˈfɪʃl] 形 人工的

obstacle [ˈɒbstəkl] 名 障碍；障碍物

device [dɪˈvaɪs] 名 设备

temperature [ˈtemprətʃə(r)] 名 温度

instant [ˈɪnstənt] 形 持续的

## Practice 请选择合适的词填在下方的横线上

assistants    imagine    temperature    control    intelligence

1. The smart home devices can automatically adjust indoor lighting and _____.

2. Artificial _____ makes computers smarter, able to solve problems like humans.

3. Can you _____ that Artificial Intelligence can help us with our work and life in the future?

4. With the help of AI _____, you can manage your daily tasks and reminders more efficiently.

5. Self-driving technology enables the vehicle to _____ itself without human intervention (干预).

## Talking practice 情景对话模拟练习

汤米对人工智能很感兴趣,他和同学黄菲菲聊起了这个话题,你也跟着练习这段对话吧。

Huang Feifei, are you using Artificial Intelligence?
黄菲菲,你在使用人工智能吗?

Tommy 汤米

Huang Feifei
黄菲菲

Yes, I use AI assistants like Xiaodu to play music.
是的,我用像小度这样的AI助手帮我播放音乐。

That's cool! Do you have any smart devices at home?
那真酷!你家里有智能设备吗?

Tommy 汤米

Huang Feifei
黄菲菲

Yes, we have smart lights and a smart air conditioner that I can control them with my voice.
有的,我们有智能灯和智能空调,我可以用语音控制它们。

Wow, can you tell me about self-driving cars in China?
哇,你能告诉我中国的自动驾驶汽车吗?

Tommy 汤米

Huang Feifei
黄菲菲

Sure! Companies like Huawei and Baidu are testing self-driving cars that can drive themselves.
当然可以!像华为和百度这样的公司正在测试可以自动驾驶的汽车。

Are there robots in hospitals, too?
医院里也有机器人吗?

Tommy 汤米

Huang Feifei
黄菲菲

Yes, smart robots help doctors by carrying medicines and showing patients where to go.
是的，智能机器人帮助医生运送药品并指引病人去哪里。

AI sounds amazing! I can't wait to see what it can do in the future.
人工智能听起来太棒了！我迫不及待想看看它在未来能做什么。

Tommy汤米

## Funny facts  关于人工智能的有趣事实和短语

**全球领导者**：中国已成为全球人工智能研究和应用的领导者之一。

**智能监控**：中国在智能监控系统中广泛应用AI技术，比如人脸识别、行为分析和公共安全管理。这些技术帮助提升了城市的安全性和管理效率。

**语音助手**：百度的"小度"（DuerOS）、阿里巴巴的"天猫精灵"（Tmall Genie）和腾讯的"叮当"（Tencent Jingle）是中国流行的语音助手，广泛应用于智能家居和移动设备中。

face recognition – 人脸识别
AI art – 人工智能艺术
AI healthcare – 人工智能医疗
AI customer service – 人工智能客服
virtual reality (VR) – 虚拟现实
AI robotics – 人工智能机器人

## Writing practice  写作小练习

根据我们这一节所学到的内容，写出下面句子的英文。

1. 自动驾驶是一种人工智能。

2. 人工智能可以帮助我们玩游戏，甚至打败最优秀的人类玩家。

3. 医院里有很多的机器人在工作。

## Reference translation 参考译文

你有没有想象过这样的情景：机器人可以帮你做家务，汽车可以自动驾驶，电脑可以理解并与你对话。这听起来像是科幻电影中的情节，但在中国，这些正在通过人工智能（AI）成为现实。

人工智能就像电脑创造的超级智慧大脑。它可以像人类一样学习、思考和解决问题。在中国，人工智能正以多种令人兴奋的方式融入生活。例如，智能机器人可以在医院帮助医生运送药物并为患者指路。有些机器人甚至可以进行简单的手术！

自动驾驶汽车是中国人工智能的另一个惊人应用。这些汽车可以在没有人类司机的情况下自行驾驶。它们使用人工智能来洞悉路况、遵守交通规则和避开障碍物。像华为和百度这样的科技公司正在街道上测试这些汽车，不久的将来，它们将成为街头巷尾的寻常风景。

在中国，还有像小度和天猫精灵这样的人工智能助手，它们可以做很多事情。它们可以回答你的问题，播放你喜欢的音乐，讲故事。这些助手就像生活在你设备中的友好帮手。

人工智能也让家庭生活变得更轻松和有趣。智能家居设备可以控制灯光、空调，甚至是厨房设备。你可以告诉你的智能音箱关灯、调节温度或开始做晚餐。这就像拥有一根魔杖，只需用你的声音就能让事情发生！

在学校里，人工智能也为学习增添了无限乐趣。有些人工智能学习应用程序可以帮助学生练习数学、学习新单词，甚至是探索科学知识。这些应用程序可以提供即时反馈和个性化课程，让学习变得更有趣且高效。

中国的人工智能文化是技术如何改善我们生活的一个美好例子。它使一切变得更智能、更轻松和更有趣。无论是医院里的机器人、自动驾驶汽车还是智能家居设备，人工智能正在把未来带到我们今天的生活中。想象一下，未来人工智能还会做哪些令人兴奋的事情吧！

# 参考答案

## Part 1 中国的历史文化

### The Imperial Palace 故宫：中国的永恒瑰宝

**Listening & Practice** 听英文原声，完成练习
1. B　　2. B　　3. B　　4. B　　5. A

**Practice** 请选择合适的词填在下方的横线上
1. allowed　　2. important　　3. World　　4. emperors　　5. take care of

**Writing Practice** 写作小练习
1. The Imperial Palace in Beijing is very big and has many rooms.
2. The Imperial Palace was built over 600 years ago and it is a cultural heritage of China.
3. Inside the Imperial Palace, you will see many beautiful artworks, as well as lovely gardens and ancient trees.

### The Terracotta Warriors 兵马俑：宏伟的"地下军团"

**Listening & Practice** 听英文原声，完成练习
1. A　　2. B　　3. C　　4. B　　5. B

**Practice** 请选择合适的词填在下方的横线上
1. statue　　2. treasures　　3. protect　　4. grand　　5. tomb

**Writing Practice** 写作小练习
1. These soldiers and horses are made of clay.
2. The tomb of Emperor Qin Shi Huang is very grand.
3. In 1974, a farmer discovered the Terracotta Warriors.

### The Mogao Grottoes 莫高窟：大漠中的艺术宫殿

**Listening & Practice** 听英文原声，完成练习
1. C　　2. B　　3. A　　4. A　　5. A

**Practice** 请选择合适的词填在下方的横线上
1. eastern　　2. UNESCO　　3. monk　　4. designed　　5. magical

### Writing Practice 写作小练习

1. The Mogao Grottoes in China are a magical place.
2. Inside the Mogao Grottoes, there are many ancient and colourful paintings.
3. Every year, many tourists come to visit the Mogao Grottoes.

## The Great Wall 长城：蜿蜒的万里巨龙

### Listening & Practice 听英文原声，完成练习

1. B  2. B  3. C  4. B  5. A

### Practice 请选择合适的词填在下方的横线上

1. messages   2. symbol   3. fixed up   4. dynasty   5. enemies

### Writing Practice 写作小练习

1. The Great Wall is a symbol of China.
2. The total length of the Great Wall is over 20,000 kilometres.
3. The watchtowers on the Great Wall were used to send messages.

## The Summer Palace 颐和园：感受皇家园林的魅力

### Listening & Practice 听英文原声，完成练习

1. B  2. B  3. C  4. B  5. B

### Practice 请选择合适的词填在下方的横线上

1. historical   2. relaxing   3. include   4. Corridor   5. royal

### Writing Practice 写作小练习

1. The Summer Palace in Beijing is a famous royal garden.
2. Kunming Lake and the Long Corridor are very famous spots in the Summer Palace.
3. Walking on the Long Corridor, you can see many wonderful Chinese paintings and beautiful lake views.

## The Yungang Grottoes 云冈石窟：巧夺天工的雕刻艺术

### Listening & Practice 听英文原声，完成练习

1. C  2. A  3. B  4. A  5. B

### Practice 请选择合适的词填在下方的横线上

1. sculptures   2. learn about   3. Grottoes   4. interesting   5. Province

### Writing Practice 写作小练习

1. The Yungang Grottoes are one of China's biggest ancient cave groups.
2. These caves attract visitors from all over the world.
3. Each cave has its own unique style, filled with many sculptures and murals.

参考答案 181

## Fujian Tulou 福建土楼：独具特色的建筑艺术

### Listening & Practice 听英文原声，完成练习
1. B  2. B  3. B  4. A  5. B

### Practice 请选择合适的词填在下方的横线上
1. buildings  2. square  3. live  4. recognized  5. traditional

### Writing Practice 写作小练习
1. The Fujian Tulou are special traditional buildings in Fujian.
2. The thick walls can resist strong winds and heavy rain, keeping the people safe.
3. These buildings are not only works of art but also a part of the local people's lives.

## Suzhou Classical Gardens 苏州古典园林：东方园林的精致之美

### Listening & Practice 听英文原声，完成练习
1. C  2. B  3. B  4. A  5. B

### Practice 请选择合适的词填在下方的横线上
1. regular  2. gardens  3. enjoy  4. twisty  5. plants

### Writing Practice 写作小练习
1. Walking in the Suzhou Gardens, you can feel a strong sense of traditional Chinese culture.
2. The rockeries, flowing water, stone bridges, and pavilions in the Suzhou Gardens make a beautiful picture.
3. The Suzhou Gardens attract many visitors with their beautiful design and unique style.

## Pingyao Ancient City 平遥古城：跨越千年的城市

### Listening & Practice 听英文原声，完成练习
1. A  2. A  3. B  4. C  5. B

### Practice 请选择合适的词填在下方的横线上
1. rebuilt  2. straight  3. banks  4. impressive  5. For example

### Writing Practice 写作小练习
1. Pingyao Ancient City is one of the best-preserved old cities in China.
2. One of China's earliest banks, Rishengchang, is in Pingyao Ancient City.
3. Pingyao Ancient City was designed to look like a turtle, so it is also called the "Turtle City".

## The Temple of Heaven 天坛：中国古代哲学思想的体现

### Listening & Practice 听英文原声，完成练习
1. A  2. B  3. B  4. B  5. C

**Practice** 请选择合适的词填在下方的横线上

1. harvests
2. all over the world
3. roof
4. temple
5. ceremony

**Writing Practice** 写作小练习

1. The Temple of Heaven is a landmark in Beijing, built during the Ming Dynasty.
2. The Hall of Prayer for Good Harvests is a big round building with a blue roof that represents the sky.
3. Emperors used to come here to pray for good harvests.

# Part 2 中国的经典艺术

## Peking Opera 京剧：当之无愧的"国粹"

**Listening & Practice** 听英文原声，完成练习

1. B    2. B    3. B    4. C    5. C

**Practice** 请选择合适的词填在下方的横线上

1. instrument    2. costumes    3. theatres    4. character    5. tricky

**Writing Practice** 写作小练习

1. Peking Opera is one of China's cultural treasures.
2. In Peking Opera, the face paint is drawn with different colours.
3. The roles in Peking Opera are divided into Sheng, Dan, Jing, and Chou.

## Chinese Painting 国画：独特的东方韵味

**Listening & Practice** 听英文原声，完成练习

1. B    2. A    3. B    4. B    5. A

**Practice** 请选择合适的词填在下方的横线上

1. brush    2. artist's    3. popular    4. painting    5. given up

**Writing Practice** 写作小练习

1. Chinese paintings often show landscapes, flowers, birds, and people.
2. Chinese paintings are made with a brush and ink on rice paper or silk.
3. Chinese paintings from different times show how people viewed nature and society back then.

## Porcelain 瓷器：让世界感到精湛的技艺

**Listening & Practice** 听英文原声，完成练习

1. B   2. B   3. B   4. C   5. A

**Practice** 请选择合适的词填在下方的横线上

1. improving   2. museum   3. porcelain   4. excellent   5. exchange

**Writing Practice** 写作小练习

1. Chinese porcelain has a history of over 2,000 years.
2. They use it to make bowls, plates, and jars.
3. You can see Chinese porcelain in many museums around the world.

## Tang and Song Poetry 唐诗宋词：中国传统的诗歌艺术

**Listening & Practice** 听英文原声，完成练习

1. A   2. C   3. B   4. C   5. B

**Practice** 请选择合适的词填在下方的横线上

1. romantic   2. literature   3. poetry   4. appreciate   5. version

**Writing Practice** 写作小练习

1. Li Bai is one of the most famous poet in Chinese history.
2. Many Tang poems are still widely known today.
3. Tang poetry often talks about nature, feelings, and social life.

## Chinese Calligraphy 书法：超越文字魅力的艺术

**Listening & Practice** 听英文原声，完成练习

1. B   2. C   3. A   4. B   5. A

**Practice** 请选择合适的词填在下方的横线上

1. scripts   2. flowing   3. patience   4. Calligraphy   5. unique

**Writing Practice** 写作小练习

1. Chinese calligraphy has different styles.
2. If you like Chinese characters, you can learn calligraphy.
3. Wang Xizhi is one of the most famous calligraphers in Chinese history.

## Chinese Tea Culture 茶文化：悠闲的生活艺术

**Listening & Practice** 听英文原声，完成练习

1. B   2. B   3. C   4. C   5. B

**Practice** 请选择合适的词填在下方的横线上

1. tastes/smells   2. health   3. tradition
4. common   5. smells/tastes

### Writing Practice 写作小练习

1. In China, drinking tea is not only a way of life but also an art.
2. Chinese tea has six types: green tea, black tea, white tea, yellow tea, oolong tea, and dark tea.
3. In Guangdong, people prefer to drink Kung Fu tea.

## Chinese Silk 丝绸：柔软高贵的典范

### Listening & Practice 听英文原声，完成练习

1. B    2. A    3. C    4. B    5. B

### Practice 请选择合适的词填在下方的横线上

1. shine    2. fabric    3. artistic    4. silkworms    5. nobles

### Writing Practice 写作小练习

1. Silk feels very soft, so it is often used to make clothing.
2. Silk is not only beautiful but also very important in culture.
3. The Silk Road was an important trade route connecting China and the West.

## Chinese Paper-cut 剪纸艺术：民间艺术的代表

### Listening & Practice 听英文原声，完成练习

1. A    2. B    3. C    4. A    5. B

### Practice 请选择合适的词填在下方的横线上

1. shapes    2. decorate    3. put up    4. festive    5. scissors

### Writing Practice 写作小练习

1. Paper-cut is a fun and ancient art.
2. Paper-cut means using scissors or a knife to cut different shapes with paper.
3. In Chinese traditional culture, the dragon represents strength, and the fish represents wealth.

# Part 3 中国的传统节日和节气

## The Spring Festival 春节：辞旧迎新又一年

### Listening & Practice 听英文原声，完成练习

1. B    2. A    3. B    4. B    5. C

**Practice** 请选择合适的词填在下方的横线上

1. sweep away  2. envelopes  3. calendar
4. dumplings  5. festival

**Writing Practice** 写作小练习

1. The Spring Festival is the start of a new year and the most important traditional festival in China.
2. During The Spring Festival, people wear new clothes and visit family and friends.
3. Children receive lucky money from their parents.

## The Lantern Festival 元宵节：团团圆圆的节日

**Listening & Practice** 听英文原声，完成练习

1. B  2. A  3. C  4. B  5. C

**Practice** 请选择合适的词填在下方的横线上

1. hang  2. togetherness  3. riddles
4. activities  5. sticky

**Writing Practice** 写作小练习

1. People walk in the streets and watch the beautiful lanterns.
2. Riddles are a traditional custom during the Lantern Festival.
3. Yuanxiao is the traditional food of the Lantern Festival.

## The Tomb-sweeping Day 清明节：祭祖踏青的好时节

**Listening & Practice** 听英文原声，完成练习

1. B  2. A  3. B  4. A  5. C

**Practice** 请选择合适的词填在下方的横线上

1. remember  2. respect  3. ancestors  4. graves  5. wakes up

**Writing Practice** 写作小练习

1. During the Tomb-sweeping Day, people go to clean the graves and pay respect to their ancestors.
2. During the Tomb-sweeping Day, people go for an outing to enjoy the beauty of nature.
3. People fly kites during the Tomb-sweeping Day to celebrate the coming of spring.

## The Dragon Boat Festival 端午节：一起来赛龙舟吧

**Listening & Practice** 听英文原声，完成练习

1. A  2. B  3. C  4. A  5. B

**Practice** 请选择合适的词填在下方的横线上

1. protection    2. wrapped    3. paddling    4. threads    5. courage

**Writing Practice** 写作小练习

1. On the Dragon Boat Festival, people hold dragon boat races to celebrate the holiday.
2. Zongzi is the traditional food of the Dragon Boat Festival, and it is made of sticky rice.
3. The Dragon Boat Festival is to commemorate a patriotic Chinese poet named Qu Yuan.

## The Mid-Autumn Festival 中秋节：每逢佳节倍思亲

**Listening & Practice** 听英文原声，完成练习

1. C    2. B    3. C    4. A    5. B

**Practice** 请选择合适的词填在下方的横线上

1. bright    2. Mooncakes    3. thankful    4. float    5. snacks

**Writing Practice** 写作小练习

1. The Mid-Autumn Festival is a holiday for family reunions.
2. People enjoy looking at the moon and eating mooncakes during the Mid-Autumn Festival.
3. Mooncakes are the traditional food of the Mid-Autumn Festival, and they are very delicious.

## Twenty-four Solar Terms 二十四节气：中国古代智慧结晶

**Listening & Practice** 听英文原声，完成练习

1. C    2. B    3. B    4. A    5. B

**Practice** 请选择合适的词填在下方的横线上

1. customs    2. Solar    3. farming    4. affects    5. store

**Writing Practice** 写作小练习

1. The Twenty-four Solar Terms started near the Yellow River in China.
2. The solar terms can help farmers plan their farming activities.
3. During the Beginning of Spring, people like to eat spring pancakes.

# Part 4 中国的现代科技和文化

## China Railway Highspeed 中国高铁：有趣又快速的出行体验

**Listening & Practice** 听英文原声，完成练习
1. A    2. C    3. B    4. B    5. A

**Practice** 请选择合适的词填在下方的横线上
1. worry about    2. electricity    3. scenery
4. ensures    5. convenience

**Writing Practice** 写作小练习
1. High-speed trains can travel at very high speeds.
2. High-speed trains are not only spacious but also very comfortable.
3. It takes only 4.5 hours to travel from Beijing to Shanghai by high-speed train.

## China's Space Exploration 中国的太空探索：追寻星辰大海

**Listening & Practice** 听英文原声，完成练习
1. B    2. C    3. A    4. B    5. C

**Practice** 请选择合适的词填在下方的横线上
1. taikonauts    2. launched    3. universe    4. surface    5. satellite

**Writing Practice** 写作小练习
1. China has made great achievements in space exploration.
2. Yang Liwei is the first Chinese taikonaut to go into space.
3. Building a bigger space station allows more taikonauts to live and work in space.

## Digital Life in China 数字生活在中国：一种新的生活方式

**Listening & Practice** 听英文原声，完成练习
1. C    2. C    3. B    4. B    5. A

**Practice** 请选择合适的词填在下方的横线上
1. Digital    2. smartphones    3. transformed    4. payment    5. deliver

**Writing Practice** 写作小练习
1. We can shop online anytime and anywhere.
2. In today's life, digital payments are fast and safe.
3. We can play games, watch movies, and listen to music through the Internet.

## New Energy Vehicles 新能源汽车：驶向未来

### Listening & Practice 听英文原声，完成练习
1. B    2. C    3. B    4. B    5. A

### Practice 请选择合适的词填在下方的横线上
1. advanced    2. decrease    3. battery    4. vehicle    5. charge

### Writing Practice 写作小练习
1. In China, new energy vehicles are very popular.
2. New energy vehicles can reduce air pollution and are good for the environment.
3. Electric vehicles do not need gasoline, they only need to be charged.

## Artificial Intelligence (AI) 人工智能：未来就在眼前

### Listening & Practice 听英文原声，完成练习
1. C    2. B    3. B    4. A    5. C

### Practice 请选择合适的词填在下方的横线上
1. temperature    2. Intelligence    3. imagine
4. assistants    5. control

### Writing Practice 写作小练习
1. Self-driving is a type of AI(artificial Intelligence).
2. AI(Artificial Intelligence) can help us play games and even beat the best human players.
3. There are many robots working in hospitals.